MW00778220

MOBSTERS, MADAMS & MURDER IN STEUBENVILLE, OHIO

THE STORY OF LITTLE CHICAGO

SUSAN M. GUY

THE
History
PRESS

Published by The History Press
Charleston, SC 29403
www.historypress.net

Front cover, far left: Vincent Caparra, killer of Mingo Junction police lieutenant William J. Snider. *Public domain photo from Ohio DRC website.*

First published 2014

ISBN 978.1.5402.1058.6

Library of Congress Cataloging-in-Publication Data

Guy, Susan M.
Mobsters, madams and murder in Steubenville, Ohio : the story of Little Chicago / Susan M. Guy.
pages cm. -- (True crime)
ISBN 978-1-62619-567-7 (paperback)
1. Organized crime--Ohio--Steubenville--History--20th century. 2. Crime--Ohio--Steubenville--Case studies. 3. Criminals--Ohio--Steubenville--Case studies. I. Title.
HV6452.O3G89 2014
364.152'3097716909042--dc23
2014017145

This book is dedicated to the Steubenville and Mingo Junction police officers and Jefferson County Prohibition dry agents who lost their lives during the "Little Chicago" days in this county. Dry agents are a forgotten branch of law enforcement when it comes to remembering those who fell in the line of duty.

CONTENTS

Contents

ACKNOWLEDGEMENTS

The following people were instrumental in helping me get this book off the ground:

Karen Majoris Garrison (Karina Garrison), author and president of the Tri State Writers Society, who encouraged me to write a short story assignment on prostitution in Steubenville. Thank you, Karen, for your guidance and support through all of this and for all of the good stuff to come.

Danice Ryan, my friend and genealogy sidekick, whose encouragement and support during this whole process has been invaluable. Thank you for being my "test reader" and letting me bend your ear.

Dave Guy Jr., my son, whose eye for photography is incredible. Thank you for letting me borrow some of your pictures and for being my son.

Thank you to my mom, Eloise Pompa, for your encouragement and support in everything I do. I inherited my love of reading and writing from you.

Thank you to my dad, retired Wintersville Police captain Robert "Red" Nottingham, from whom I inherited a love for law enforcement.

INTRODUCTION

"If you want to commit a murder and get away with it, just go to Jefferson County, Ohio." That's a phrase that I grew up hearing all my life. I never really knew the reason behind it, and I'm sure that the people saying it probably didn't know either. Whispers of mobsters, madams and unsolved murders floated around for decades, but nobody wanted to come right out and talk about it. The mob, Water Street madams and unsolved murders were topics that interested me. To dig up the past and tie it all together in one book seemed like a challenge, but I didn't realize what a huge challenge it would be. Too many murders and other crimes were coming to the surface—too many to cover in one book. The Prohibition era was a headline-making time for Steubenville and all of Jefferson County.

Steubenville, the county seat of Jefferson County, Ohio, lies on the banks of the Ohio River, with the West Virginia Panhandle towns of Weirton and Follansbee directly east, across the river. Wellsburg, West Virginia, is just south of Follansbee, and Pittsburgh, Pennsylvania, is thirty-eight miles east of Steubenville. Cleveland, Columbus and Youngstown are a couple hours away by car. Steubenville's location will become important as you delve into the stories within the covers of this book. It has had a knack for gaining negative worldwide attention for over one hundred years. The number of murders that occurred within its corporation limits during Prohibition was far too many for a town of its size. Convictions for murders during that time were rare. In the early 1920s, this negative attention earned it the nickname of "Little Chicago" by the national press. It's an unwelcomed reputation that the city has been unable to shake, as history seems to keep repeating itself. The small towns that dot the countryside throughout Jefferson County were not spared this reputation, either.

The 1890s through the 1900s saw a rise in Steubenville's murders and other major criminal activities, such as gambling, bootlegging and prostitution. Ohio had already become the major target of the Anti-Saloon League and the Woman's Christian Temperance Union. Citizens of Steubenville started their own chapters of these two organizations to try to close down over 80 saloons within the city limits and over 140 throughout Jefferson County. They believed that liquor was the cause for a decline in morals and family values and wanted the manufacture and distribution of it stopped. Without the evil influence of alcohol, it was believed that this deluge of immoral behavior would cease, once and for all, and peace would come to Jefferson County.

In the 1910s, '20s and '30s, allegations of political corruption arose, as vice crimes appeared to be overlooked or given light fines by city and county officials. The corruption and lack of convictions for major crimes caused the fully hooded members of the Ku Klux Klan chapter from just across the river in Wellsburg, West Virginia, to make their first appearance in the city. Twelve local ministers joined forces against the violence and corruption in Steubenville in the 1940s, and their story was documented in the 1947 book *Twelve Against the Underworld.*

In spite of their valiant fight, the tarnished image of the city didn't get any cleaner in the years to come. In the late 1960s, Madam Judy Jordan made front-page news after being given an alleged uniformed bodyguard from the sheriff's department. She would serve her jail sentences at the Ohio Valley Hospital instead of in a jail cell. Her miraculous recovery from a mysterious illness would coincide with the day that her jail sentence was up. Unsurprisingly, her client list contained many notable men.

In 1970, Steubenville was named one of the top ten dirtiest cities in the United States. It was dirty because the steel mills, power plants and other industries were working full steam ahead, and the city was prospering. People were gainfully employed, and sons and daughters followed in their parents' footsteps by working at the local steel mills. Now the steel mills have gone by the wayside, and Steubenville is fighting to find itself once again. It became cleaner, thanks to government regulations, but the young people started moving away to find jobs elsewhere.

In the 1990s, the Steubenville Police Department came under fire for numerous civil rights lawsuits filed against it, and the federal government stepped in to investigate. As a result of the findings, Steubenville, Ohio, became the second city in the United States to sign a consent decree. Under the decree, the city agreed to give its officers more training, to implement new guidelines and to add an internal affairs division to oversee any alleged wrongdoings.

Steubenville's proximity to larger cities in the tri-state area and Interstate 70 has made it a hub for drug runners. Shootings, mostly drug-related, occur on an all-too-frequent basis, leaving the local citizens to wonder *when*, not *if*, the next shooting will happen. This is reminiscent of the Prohibition era, when rumrunning was the shoot-'em-up crime of the day.

The good people of Steubenville are in the process of revitalizing the city. It has undergone many wonderful renovations, with new industries coming to the area. Descendants of the people from the "Little Chicago" era are doing their ornery ancestors proud. The gas and oil industry is pumping new life and promise into the area as Steubenville's citizens struggle to make it shine, like the historic gateway to the west it once was.

Within the pages of this book, you will find stories about some of the people and events of Steubenville and Jefferson County's "Little Chicago" days. The stories are simply a collection of historical facts taken from the pages of the *Steubenville Herald-Star, Steubenville Weekly Gazette* and other newspapers from across the nation that carried its infamous escapades. It is a remembrance of these people, regardless of how they lived their lives. Most are of prohibition crimes, though some are just interesting tales of that era. They are worth remembering and retelling and are not meant to offend anyone but are simply to remind us that today is no different from yesteryear. The *Steubenville Herald-Star* has been in existence for over two hundred years. The Schiappa Library Genealogy Room keeps the newspaper on microfilm, where I was able to research many of the facts. Using a couple well-known genealogy websites, I was able to do a background on many of these people to enlighten myself and the reader about what their lives were like.

The number of dry agents murdered during Prohibition is a record that Jefferson County, Ohio, unfortunately, holds. This made it a nationwide target for the media and gave it the unwanted nickname of "Little Chicago." My hope is that maybe we can learn something from the past to help change the future instead of trying to bury it. I hope you enjoy the stories within this book as much as I've enjoyed researching them.

PART I

1900 TO 1920:
PRE-PROHIBITION ERA

CHAPTER 1

MURDER AT THE PARK HOUSE RESORT

The 1800s were a prosperous time in Steubenville's history, as industries flourished and river traffic was heavy along the banks of the Ohio. Captains of the vessels doing trade from Pittsburgh to Cincinnati and Chicago needed somewhere along the line to pull into port and allow their crews to relax and have fun. Steubenville's Water Street provided all a sailor could ask for. Known as the red-light or tenderloin district, Water Street was lined with resorts and houses of ill fame. The two major resorts were Park House and Ohio Valley House.

Park House, owned by William May Horner, was a saloon, parlor, rooming house and whorehouse in one. It did a booming business and changed hands many times over the years, often due to the owners' brushes with the law. The dark-haired, debonair Horner was no stranger to the law, having been arrested numerous times over the years for public drunkenness. In 1887, he was fined for selling intoxicating liquor to a minor. Later the same year, he was charged with interfering with city fireman Frank Weaver while Weaver was trying to put out a house fire. He was fined thirty-two dollars by Mayor Henry Opperman for the offense.

On April 12, 1900, while loud patrons filled the first-floor saloon and parlor with their drinking and gambling, William Horner and his beautiful wife, Barbara, were upstairs in their living quarters. Barbara, known as Maude to the girls, had allegedly been bedridden with mumps for the past few days. The couple had recently been indicted by the grand jury for operating a house of ill fame and faced time in the Canton workhouse.

Above: Steubenville, Ohio, taken from across the Ohio River in Brooke County, West Virginia. In the foreground is Water Street, the infamous red-light district. *Postcard from the collection of Susan Guy. Printed by the Hugh C. Leighton Company of Portland, Maine.*

Left: William May Horner, the Park House resort owner who killed his wife. *From the* Steubenville Herald, *March 1900. Used with permission.*

Horner had been in the workhouse previously. Once, he'd even fled across the river to West Virginia to avoid prosecution.

A few minutes past 11:00 p.m., bartender "Big Jack" MacDonald thought he heard a shot come from upstairs. A few minutes later, he heard three taps on the floorboards overhead. That had been a prearranged signal between Jack and Mrs. Horner in case she needed anything. As he headed into the parlor, he saw Mrs. Horner with both hands clutching her neck, staggering to the bottom of the staircase. Jack caught her as she fainted and noticed the gunshot wound under her right earlobe. "My God, she's been shot!" he exclaimed. He laid her on the parlor floor in front of the horrified patrons and then ran outside to find help. Twenty-four-year-old Stella Gibson, one of the three prostitutes working in the parlor, noticed Maude Horner's eyes rolling as she lay bleeding on the floor. While everyone else fled in terror, Stella's eyes welled up as she knelt and cradled Maude's head in her hands. The sweet aroma of lilacs, Maude's signature perfume, enveloped Stella as she whispered, "Can I do anything for you, Maude, to make you more comfortable?"

"I'll do something for you if you don't get out of here!" a menacing voice warned. Stella glanced up and saw a glassy-eyed Will Horner, wearing nothing but his blue underclothes, glaring at her wildly. He had a revolver leveled at her head. She screamed, raised her hands in front of her face and jumped up. Running through the parlor toward the kitchen, she looked back to see Horner kneel by his wife's head. She saw him talking to the still body, but the only thing Stella heard was "Maude."

Still somewhat unfamiliar with the layout of Park House, Stella reached the cellar door and descended the steps. She hid there for what seemed like an eternity. Heavy footsteps started down into the cellar. They stopped and then retreated. A few minutes later, she could hear what sounded like something being dragged across the floor. Stella scurried from the cellar after hearing a few moments of silence from above. She dashed out the back door, climbing over the back fence and continued running until she saw Officer Ed Zimmerman. He had arrived about 11:10 p.m. after being alerted by the bartender. "Ed! Ed!" she yelled, recognizing the familiar patrolman. "Will Horner shot Maude," Stella continued, gasping for breath. "She's lying in the parlor. He's still in there!" With the shaken woman clinging to his coattails, Zimmerman tried to get inside through the front door, but it was locked. Walking around the building, he tried to find an open door. Stella led him to the back fence where she had previously made her escape. They climbed over it and entered through the rear hall door, which was still half open. As they crept through the bar toward the parlor, Zimmerman could see Mrs. Horner's body on the floor. He unlocked the barroom doors, and stepped outside, blowing his whistle to summon assistance. Coroner George Campbell had just arrived on the train from Mingo. Upon hearing the whistle from the C&P station next door, he came running.

Zimmerman enlightened the coroner about the murder. Campbell stepped inside Park House to examine the body, noting that Mrs. Horner's robe had been pulled up to her waist and her left stocking pulled down. He also noticed a number of bruises on her face and other parts of her body. It looked like she had suffered many beatings in the past. Some of the bruises were old ones. Stella told both men that Mrs. Horner's body had been moved from where she had originally fallen. "Maude always kept money in her stocking," she added.

Officer Zimmerman telephoned for Dr. Elliott and more officers. While they waited, Zimmerman sat on the arm of the sofa, conversing with the coroner. Suddenly, the parlor curtain opened, and William Horner appeared, a strong odor of liquor emanating from him. He was now clad in a t-shirt and trousers with his right hand tucked into the waistband. Zimmerman leaped from the couch and tried to grab his wrists. Horner pulled a revolver out of the waistband and shoved the barrel against Zimmerman's face, cutting the officer's nose in the process. Coroner Campbell sprang into action, grabbing at the gun. They wrestled for control of the weapon, and Campbell won, but not before Horner shoved him through a large plate-glass window. Zimmerman tackled Horner and slapped the handcuffs on him. "I'm in for it anyhow, and I'd a shot you, too," Horner told him.

"Billy, I'm sorry this had to happen," Zimmerman mumbled, having known Horner for years. Horner hung his head and didn't reply. As the officer began tossing his club back and forth from hand to hand, Horner piped up, "You son of a bitch, you better not hit me with that thing!" He seemed perfectly sober as he was led outside to be transported to the lockup. Once they arrived at the jail, however, the barefoot Horner struggled with officers. He struck jailer John Banks in the face as he was being searched. After putting him in a cell, police continued their investigation. It was learned that Horner had gone to Tonner's Hardware Store the day before the shooting and purchased a revolver. He'd told the owner that he expected to be going to the workhouse in a few days. Scratching his head, Mr. Tonner said, "Well, what do you need with a gun then?" An odd expression had come over Horner's face, according to Tonner, who said, "He remained silent as he completed his purchase and left the store."

Word spread around Steubenville and Jefferson County about the murder of Barbara Horner, and opinions formed quickly. It was widely known that Will Horner had a tremendous jealous streak when it came to his lovely wife.

On April 15, 1900, Easter Sunday, a crowd of family and friends gathered at Union Cemetery to pay their final respects to the woman whose life had ended so tragically. A three-foot cross, made entirely of Easter lilies, stood out among the massive mound of flowers. It was her children's final gift to their mother. William Horner was not allowed to leave jail for the funeral.

Barbara "Maude" Horner, wife of William M. Horner. *From the* Steubenville Herald, *March 1900. Used with permission.*

On April 20, a special grand jury convened to hear the evidence gathered in the murder case. Mrs. Horner's eldest daughter from a previous marriage, Margaret, testified that Will Horner had shot at her mother once before. The incident happened a few years earlier when the family lived at the Ohio Valley House, another well-known resort of ill fame that Horner used to own. It came to light that the victim had suffered many beatings at the hands of her second husband but never told anyone. This confirmed the coroner's theory. Margaret explained that many nights, her mother was locked out of the Park House after being beaten, and she spent those nights at the C&P train station next door.

The raven-haired beauty had been married to Will Horner for twelve years. Much of that time she was unhappy, but she loved him so much that she never complained. It was surmised that he killed her to keep her from going to the workhouse and then was going to turn the gun on himself. Apparently, he couldn't go through with the second half of his plan.

The grand jury indicted Horner, and the trial was set for June 25, 1900. Over eighty citizens of Jefferson County were interviewed for the jury. It was the longest attempt to seat a jury in Steubenville's history. Many people knew the couple or at least knew of them and had already made up their minds as to the defendant's guilt. On June 27, a jury of twelve was finally seated, and the first-degree murder trial of William Horner began. Defense attorneys

Henry Gregg and John M. Cook asked that the jury be taken immediately to Park House to view the scene of the crime. This was done at the defendant's request, and he was taken along, escorted by the sheriff and a deputy. It was the first time that Horner had been to Park House since the fateful night, but he showed no outward signs of nervousness. He roamed about freely and then sat at the bar, leisurely smoking a cigar.

The trial lasted for four days, and numerous witnesses testified for the prosecution, among them Officers Ed Zimmerman and Lafayette Mercer and hotel owner Moses Fleetwood Walker. Walker, famous for being the first black player in major league baseball, had been walking by the Park House just as the fatal shot was fired. Fifty-six witnesses testified for the defense, most of them neighbors of Horner's father, who testified that they always saw Will and Barbara Horner together and they seemed happy. The case was handed over to the jury on Saturday at 2:35 p.m. It took less than six hours to come to a unanimous agreement. The courthouse bell rang at 8:00 p.m. to alert the waiting crowd in the streets that the verdict was in. At 8:08, the verdict of guilty of murder in the first degree, with a recommendation of life with mercy, was announced. The crowded courthouse and the city streets erupted in a thunderous roar. Margaret Horner, the defendant's mother, collapsed as the verdict was read. Mr. and Mrs. John Doerr, the parents of Barbara Horner, quietly left the courtroom, while Augustus Horner, a noted Civil War veteran, tearfully hugged his son. An emotionless Horner was escorted back to his jail cell to await the long trip to his new home at the Ohio State Penitentiary.

While the citizens of Steubenville were glad that a murderer was off the streets, those who knew William Horner before he got into the illicit activities associated with liquor remembered what an intelligent man he used to be. He had once worked at La Belle Iron Works and had been a master at his job, but the effects of alcohol led him astray. He'd even invented a new kind of bolt needed for a piece of equipment at the Iron Works. The patent for that bolt made him a wealthy man. Friends and well-wishers hoped he would find a good job in the prison and stay out of trouble.

On July 12, 1900, when Horner was told he'd be leaving for Columbus the next morning, he asked the jailer to send for a barber. He had his hair cut short and shaved off his mustache. The handsome thirty-four-year-old man looked like an innocent boy after the barber had finished.

The last visit between Horner and his family was emotional for everyone in the room. His wall of pent-up emotions finally crumbled as he hugged and kissed his children. The whimpering offspring clung to his neck, not wanting to let go. Their paternal grandparents had to pull the children away, as they, too, said their tearful good-byes.

The sheriff chose to take his prisoner to the penitentiary on the 3:00 a.m. train. The train station was empty at that time of the morning, so they got underway to Columbus without any hoopla.

While serving his life sentence at Ohio's maximum-security prison, Horner was a model inmate. Numerous attempts at a new trial were squashed. In April 1910, the warden gave him a trustee job running the prison's pump station.

In 1915, his youngest daughter, Barbara, who had been asleep at the time of the murder, petitioned the judge, stating that her father was very ill and needed to be home. Horner had convinced the girl that he didn't murder her mother, and she believed him. The judge agreed to her petition, and Horner was released after serving fifteen years in prison. Soon after his release, he married Mildred Nixon Phillips and resided in Mt. Vernon, Ohio, for years. Three of his children with first wife, Barbara, had married three of Mildred's children. His second wife returned to Steubenville and divorced Horner in 1932, while he was still

The monument at Union Cemetery in Steubenville, Ohio, marking the final resting place of William Horner and some of his children. *Photo by Susan Guy.*

living in Mt. Vernon. He died of lung cancer in Steubenville in 1937, and is buried in Union Cemetery with his family and his wife, Barbara. William M. Horner's name is prominently displayed on a monument, with no dates. His first wife's grave has no marker.

CHAPTER 2

MURDER FOR LOVE

In August 1900, the people of Steubenville were anxious to move on from the grim notoriety of the William Horner murder trial that had consumed them for the past few months. With the convicted wife-killer safely tucked away in the state prison, many locals were looking forward to the August 16 wedding of two former Steubenville residents, Rosslyn Ferrell and his sweetheart, Lillian Costlow. Ross was the youngest son of bridge contractor Tobias Ferrell and his wife, Anna. Ross's handsome, slender, six-foot frame caught the eye of many a young lady in Steubenville, but his eye saw only Lillian. She was the beautiful daughter of railroad engineer Patrick Costlow and had moved with her parents to Columbus two years earlier. Ross followed a year later. He had been employed by Adams Express Company in Steubenville since August 1897 as a transfer clerk. In May 1899, he was promoted to messenger on the road. He worked on the Pittsburgh to Columbus train, which allowed him to travel between Steubenville and Columbus, thus being able to see his family. The two sweethearts were counting the days until their lavish wedding. Their Steubenville friends and family were busy packing for the wedding event of the year.

On August 10, 1900, newspapers across Ohio were emblazoned with the headlines, "Adams Express Messenger Fatally Shot." The victim, Charles Lane, was well known to people in Columbus. The married father of one worked the line between Columbus and St. Louis, Missouri. His body was discovered in the express car as the train pulled into Columbus just after midnight.

"Thank goodness it wasn't Ross," Tobias Ferrell sighed, as he sat across the dinner table from his wife, reading the *Steubenville Herald*. "What a sad thing! He left a wife and small child," Anna replied. "I believe Ross mentioned Charles Lane once or twice. Well, Papa, we won't worry about that horrible story anymore. We've got a wedding to pack for! Lord knows, we need a little happiness around here!" Tobias agreed, looking ruefully down at his leg. He'd injured it a few months before, when he fell from a beam on the Market Street Bridge job. The couple switched their conversation to their son's wedding six days away.

At 11:40 p.m. on Friday, August 10, 1900, Adams Express employees J.M. Sheldon and Charles Ausburg were unable to get into car 208 after it pulled into Union Depot in Columbus. It was locked. They shouted to Lane to open the door. Getting no reply, the two men started to get worried. "That's not like Charlie," Sheldon said. He and Ausburg tried the doors at the ends of the car. One of them was ajar, so they entered the car, with lanterns in hand. The men weren't prepared for the ghastly sight that greeted them in the dim yellow glow. Twenty-eight-year-old Charles Lane was lying face down in a crimson puddle, his body riddled with bullets. His corncob pipe lay on the floor just beyond the reach of his stilled fingers. Blood splattered the walls, and papers were scattered about. Both men backed slowly outside, in a state of shock. They spread the word throughout the station that Lane had been murdered. Authorities were called to the scene. Columbus police chief W.P. Tyler and Inspector Thomas Baron arrived within a few minutes, bringing all available officers with them. A crowd began to gather, swarming the depot. Dr. William Birmingham, the Franklin County coroner, arrived a few minutes later. After a quick examination of the body at the scene, he stated, "Mr. Lane was shot seven times." He dug a few slugs out of the body. "They're all from a .38 caliber revolver," he continued. "Three shots went into the right leg, three in the right side, with one puncturing the heart, and two passing through the lungs. Another shot went into his left side." Detective Thomas O'Neill found another shell that had gone wild, embedding itself into the floor. The men surmised that two robbers must have entered the car, until Detective O'Neill found a .38 caliber revolver lying inside the way safe, beside an envelope full of money that must have been overlooked by the thieves. "That's Charlie Lane's revolver," express messenger Sheldon volunteered. "Charlie always carried it with him, and it was always loaded." Detective O'Neill opened the cylinder, revealing four unspent cartridges and two that were fired. "Well, there's our eight shots, boys," O'Neill said, as he showed the cylinder to his fellow detectives, James Dundon and Thomas J. Foster. O'Neill examined the contents of the way safe further and found a folded piece of paper inside. "Jim, what do you make of this?" He passed the paper to Dundon, who read it aloud, "If I am rendered unconscious or killed, my name is Charles Lane. I reside at 244 Fourth Avenue, Columbus, Ohio. My age is twenty-eight, 130 pounds; height, five feet, nine and a half inches."

The note was dated June 19, 1900. "Spooky, isn't it?" Foster shivered. "I wonder if he had a premonition or something." The three veteran Columbus police officers were bound and determined to solve the most horrific murder case they had ever worked on and find the person or persons responsible for getting away with an undetermined amount of money, jewels and other valuables. Who could this monster be? That was the question on the minds of everyone involved in the case.

The train on which the murder occurred consisted of one passenger car, three mail cars and the express car where the body was found. Dundon questioned the baggage master, John Fletcher. "When did you last see Lane?" he asked.

Fletcher replied, "The last time I saw him alive was in Urbana, when we took on baggage. I was in the car ahead of him." Fletcher thought for a minute and then added, "At Cable, I heard some men talking outside. I couldn't understand what they were saying."

"Was there anything suspicious about the men?" Dundon asked.

Fletcher responded, "No, sir, I didn't hear or see anything more until after we passed Plain City."

Dundon pressed the baggage master, "What happened then?"

Fletcher replied, "I went to wash up, and tried to get into the express car, but something heavy appeared to be up against the door. I thought it must have been freight, so I walked away."

Dundon turned his attention to the conductor, Jerry Taylor, asking, "When did you last see Lane alive?"

"Well, Lane and I were friends, and we talked often during the St. Louis to Columbus run. He stuck his head out of the car and waved at me as we approached Milford Center," Taylor answered. The three detectives looked at one another. Foster was the first to speak. "Well, our victim was alive as the train pulled into Milford Center. That narrows the field quite a bit," he said. "Yes, indeed!" O'Neill replied. "Maybe we're getting somewhere now."

It was after two in the morning when Detectives O'Neill, Dundon and Foster jumped on a westbound train to Plain City. At stops along the way, they questioned railroad employees, gathering information. When they arrived at Plain City, they rented a horse and buggy from the liveryman. They questioned him but didn't get anywhere. "Maybe we should check that hotel," O'Neill suggested, pointing to a building not far from the train station. Dundon nodded in agreement, and the three men rode toward the Smiley House, hoping for a break in their case. They tied their horse and buggy up to the hitching post and walked inside.

"Hello, gentlemen," the desk clerk greeted them. "I'm W.B. Smiley, the owner. Would you like a room? We're the only hotel in town."

"No, sir, we'd just like to ask you a few questions, if you don't mind. These men are Detectives O'Neill and Foster, and I'm Detective Dundon with the Columbus Police Department," the officer began. "Did you have any guests register here last night?"

"No sir, I don't recall anybody coming in last night. I'm sorry I can't be of any help," Smiley replied. "What are you looking for, may I ask?"

"An Adams Express messenger was murdered last night, and we have reason to believe the killer may have gotten off the train here," O'Neill answered. "If you remember anything that can help us, please get in touch." Foster glanced around the room, observing a copy of the *St. Louis Republic* newspaper, dated August 10, and a paper containing the names and addresses of two persons from Columbus lying on a table. Thinking these items may be of importance to their case, he grabbed them up as evidence. The officers then left the hotel. St. Louis to Columbus was the route taken by murder victim, Charles Lane. Armed with this possible new clue, the men got in their buggy and headed toward Milford Center, where Lane was last seen alive.

They arrived at Milford Center station later in the afternoon on August 11. Patrick Dea, the station agent, greeted them. The detectives asked him if he'd seen Charles Lane last night.

"Yes, I did," Dea replied. "I waved and called out to him. A.J. Cashdollar, a freight conductor from another train that was waiting on a siding, glimpsed another man in the car with Lane, as it went by. He just mentioned it to me in passing."

With this valuable piece of information, the three men drove back toward Plain City, theorizing about what had happened during the previous night's brutal crime. Someone who Lane knew, perhaps an Adams Express employee, or former employee, talked Lane into letting him ride in the car. The unknown man used his friendship as a ploy to rob and kill the young express messenger. Back in Plain City, the detectives returned to the Smiley House, remembering the newspaper and cards that they'd found there. To their surprise, Mr. Smiley greeted them, somewhat sheepishly, "I'm sorry, gentlemen, but after you left, I remembered a young man, wearing a white fedora and light gray suit, who came in late last night and took a room." Smiley went on, "I was so tired that I forgot to give him the sign-in register."

"Can you remember anything else?" Dundon asked, his voice betraying a bit of excitement.

"Yes, he ate his breakfast and paid his bill and then asked my wife for some wrapping cord to mail a parcel." Smiley continued, "He was a good-looking young man. Had dark hair and eyes and said his name was Kaler." Mrs. Smiley added, "It was a brown paper parcel. Mr. Kaler didn't want any help with it, though I offered to wrap it for him."

"Show me his room," Foster demanded. Mrs. Smiley led him upstairs to the suspect's room, while Dundon and O'Neill made a few phone calls and then headed back to Columbus by train. Upon reaching Union Station, they learned that police already had the suspicious package in their possession and had it unwrapped. Inside were money orders and wrappers, along with waybills, containing the signature of Charles Lane. The men were closing in on their suspect.

At the Smiley House, Foster found a .38-caliber revolver stuffed under a pillow. Its cylinder contained six fired shell casings. After finding a few money orders and wrappers overlooked by the killer, an elated Foster departed Smiley House and jumped on the next train for Columbus. Dundon and O'Neill pressed on at Union Station, asking about the man in the white fedora. Finally, one of the station employees spoke up and pointed toward a bench, saying, "A young man wearing a white fedora sat over there reading a book. He kept looking at the clock, like he was waiting for a train." The employee continued, "He looked vaguely familiar. I think he worked for Adams Express a few months ago."

The detectives' hearts raced with the new information. Their hunch had been right all along. They just needed to find out how many former Adams Express employees lived on the north side of Columbus. They persisted in their questioning of employees at Union Station until one name came to light, that of Rosslyn Ferrell. He'd lost his job in June.

On Sunday, August 12, Dundon and O'Neill knocked on the door of a rooming house on West Goodale Street. A woman opened the door, saying, "Yes, can I help you?" After identifying themselves, O'Neill asked, "Does Rosslyn Ferrell room here?"

"Why, yes, he does, but he's not here right now," the landlady replied. The woman identified herself as Laura Montfort, wife of Adams Express messenger J.C. Montfort.

"We'd like to question him about a robbery," said Dundon.

"Mr. Ferrell, a thief!" She exclaimed. "I hardly think so! He's a gentleman."

"May we take a look at his room, please?" the detective asked.

"Sure, sure," she replied. "You'll see for yourself that Ross is no criminal."

Mrs. Montfort led Dundon and O'Neill to Ferrell's room. O'Neill opened the closet door, and staring back at him were a light gray suit and white fedora. Both men felt a slight rush and knew they had found their man.

"Now that I think of it," Mrs. Montford said, "Ross was in his room a couple nights ago. It sounded like he was clicking the cylinder of a revolver." She went on, "He's from Steubenville, you know. He's getting married on Thursday, to Miss Lillian Costlow."

"What!" Dundon cried. "Not Patrick Costlow's daughter?"

"Yes! Do you know them?" Mrs. Montfort asked, noting the dismayed look on the detective's face.

"Thank you, Mrs. Montfort. We've found all we need here," Dundon mumbled. The detectives made their exit, meeting up with Foster a short time later to compare findings. Dundon and Costlow attended the same church and were friends. This was going to be a tough one for the seasoned detective.

More pieces of the puzzle fell into place as the detectives traced Ross Ferrell's movements over the previous two days. He had paid a couple of his old landlords for back rent the day after the murder, in cash. For an unemployed messenger, Ferrell had suddenly come into a lot of money.

Dundon and O'Neill rode past the Costlow home, parking their buggy down the street. They spied the young couple sitting on a blanket in the backyard. Lillian was gazing at her handsome bridegroom, listening intently, as he whispered in her ear. Knowing that their unexpected appearance was about to change two young lives forever, the detectives approached the ill-fated pair. "Rosslyn Ferrell?" O'Neill asked.

"Yes," he smiled. "Excuse me, Lillie. I believe these gentlemen would like to have a word with me." Ross stood up and walked a few yards away with the detectives.

"Mr. Ferrell, we're with the Columbus Police Department," said O'Neill. "We'd like to ask you a few questions about a robbery. Would you come with us to headquarters?"

Still smiling, Ferrell replied, "Please wait until I speak with my fiancé so she won't worry." After a few words with his shocked bride, Ferrell willingly went with the officers to police headquarters as if nothing in the world was wrong.

Upon arrival at the station, the officers' demeanor changed. "Mr. Ferrell, you weren't brought here to be questioned about a robbery. You were brought in for the murder of Charles Lane." Dundon showed no mercy on the lad as he continued, "We know you murdered him, so you might as well confess." O'Neill took up the barrage of questioning. "We intercepted the parcel you mailed out, containing money orders and wrappers with Lane's signature on them."

Ferrell only shrugged his shoulders. "The only thing I know is what I read in the newspapers."

"Well, maybe you'll confess after you've cooled your heels in a cell for a while," retorted Dundon. They escorted Ross to a dark cell in the basement of the jail and left him alone. A few hours later, he yelled for the detectives, ready to confess his crime. The dark solitude had unnerved the cocky youth.

"Come on, Ross," coaxed Dundon. "Let's have it."

"I killed Lane and took the money. I'd lost my job a few months back and was desperate," Ross began. "I had looked for another job but couldn't find one. Lillie and I were soon to be married, and I needed to take care of her."

"What did you do with the money?" O'Neill pressed.

"I bought some new clothes, paid some bills and gave some to Lillie," said Ross. At that moment, the young bridegroom suddenly broke down and sobbed. It was as if the realization of the severity of his crime had just hit him. "Please save me! I will be put to death for this!" he cried. For an instant, the officers almost felt sorry for him. It was such a heartbreaking sight. They could only imagine what the scene would be like at the Costlow home that night once Ross's confession reached the family. He was taken to Chief Tyler's office, where he gave a complete, matter-of-fact account of his crime. He told it in such a cold, unremorseful manner that the officers could see his dual personality emerge. Their killer was a true psychopath.

"Please send for Lillie; I'd like to see her," Ross asked the detectives.

"We'll see," Dundon replied, as a jailer led the young man back to his cell. They returned to the Costlow home, where a gloomy atmosphere greeted them. A grim-looking Patrick Costlow answered the door. Dundon and O'Neill knew that news of Ferrell's confession had preceded them to the residence.

"Lillie is lying down. I'm sure you can understand that she doesn't want to talk to anyone right now," Costlow said.

"Pat, we have to talk to her. The sooner we get it over with, the sooner we'll get out of your hair," Dundon told his friend.

"I guess you're right, Jim," Costlow replied. "If Ross needed a job or money, all he had he to do was come to me. I'd have done anything for him and my little girl." The heartsick father started sobbing uncontrollably, as Dundon and O'Neill felt their own eyes getting moist.

"Take it easy, Pat," Dundon patted his shoulder. "Lillie's a tough young lady. She'll get through this, but we still need to talk to her."

Overhearing the conversation, Mrs. Julia Costlow, her face puffy from crying, walked into the room and greeted the men. "Hi, Jim. I'll go get Lillie for you," she said.

Ten minutes later, a visibly shaken Lillie was led into the front room by her mother, who helped her into a chair. "Lillie, I'm so sorry for what's happened, but we have to talk to you," Dundon started. "Did you know anything about this?"

"No, I didn't know anything. I thought Ross was still working for the express company," she cried. "He gave me over $900 yesterday and told me to put it in the bank. He said he'd saved it for our marriage."

On August 13, Ross Ferrell's murder confession splashed across the front pages of newspapers across the nation. The *Steubenville Herald-Star* was no different, as Ross's boyish face stared back at his family and friends from the front page. His mother collapsed and was bedridden. Her other boys were in disbelief that their brother could do such a thing. They were afraid that their mother wouldn't recover from the shock. Tobias Ferrell made arrangements to see his son. Once again, Steubenville had been thrust in a negative spotlight as newspapers picked up on the fact that Lane's killer was originally from that city.

Accompanied by her father, Lillie visited her ill-fated love in his jail cell. The young woman, attired in black, whispered words meant for his ears only. The weakened Ferrell sank to his cot, completely drained of energy. Lillie gave him a final long, passionate kiss and then made her exit.

Authorities were unsure if jurisdiction for the crime fell within Champaign or Union County. Ferrell helped them with that fact, stating he had murdered Lane in Union County. Cops had to bodily carry the severely weak and depressed Ferrell to the paddy wagon, amid angry crowds gathered at the Columbus jail. The mob scene was repeated again at Marysville. At the Union County jail, they put him in a lone cell on the women's block. Some said it was because the men's side was overcrowded, while others claim it was for the pretty boy's protection. He was placed on suicide watch.

As his notoriety grew, the sickly Ferrell rallied. His cocky alter ego reappeared, relishing the fact that he was in the nation's limelight. The doomed ex-bridegroom even grew a mustache. Young schoolgirls gathered outside his barred jailhouse window, leaving mounds of flowers and gifts, until the irate sheriff ran them off.

Ross Ferrell was indicted on September 12, and his trial followed quickly thereafter. He sent a letter to Lillie, telling her that he would come out of it just fine. He truly believed he wouldn't be convicted. His fiancé and her parents visited him the day before the trial. The conversation was light and jolly. It was the first time that Patrick Costlow had spoken to Ferrell since he'd been taken into custody.

The Union County Courthouse was packed to capacity with curious onlookers. Ferrell looked around the room for Lillie. He spied his frail mother and quickly turned away, his eyes unable to meet hers.

Though testimony was given by a number of witnesses, none caused a greater flurry of excitement than that of Ferrell's sweetheart. Lillie Costlow made her way to the stand and answered every question matter-of-factly, avoiding her lover's gaze. When she was done, he became quite unnerved. At the end of the court session, he had to be led to his cell and given a sedative.

In his closing arguments of the trial, Union County prosecutor Campbell stated that Miss Costlow was a very fortunate lady, having narrowly escaped the clutches of such a monster.

Members of the jury were sent out as all residents living in the state of Ohio awaited the verdict. Shortly after midnight, they returned with a verdict of guilty of murder in the first degree. Ferrell's mother and sweetheart both fainted, as he screamed, "I'll never go to that chair!" Taking this as a threat to commit suicide or escape, he was placed on watch until he left for the Ohio Penitentiary. A motion for retrial was overruled by the judge, who sentenced Ferrell to death in the electric chair.

His final day on earth was spent writing letters to his two favorite ladies, his mother and Lillie. He expressed his love to the

Rosslyn "Ross" Ferrell, who killed Adams Express messenger Charles Lane in 1900. *Photograph courtesy Ohio DRC website. Public domain.*

Grave marker of Rosslyn Ferrell located in Union Cemetery in Steubenville. *Photo by Susan Guy.*

fiancée for whom he had killed and bid her farewell. The letter to his mother outlined his final wishes, including a request to line his casket with his favorite color. After asking the guard to mail his final communications, he sat down and strummed a guitar.

On March 1, 1901, he calmly walked to the chair, attired in the gray suit and brightly colored tie that he had purchased with ill-gotten money. With a smile on his lips, the switch was flipped. Lillie and Mrs. Ferrell witnessed the execution and then brought Ross home.

His body was removed to the funeral home on West Market Street in Steubenville, where he was laid out in a fine casket, surrounded by hundreds of flowers. Police controlled the mob out on the sidewalk, making way for the mourners to enter. Adorned in a long black veil, Lillie sobbed uncontrollably, as she looked down at Ross for the last time. "I love you," she whispered. He looked as if he would awake at any second and answer back, "I love you, too, Lillie." How handsome he looked against the purple brocade.

Eight months later, Lillie was married to a man who had seen her photograph in the newspaper in connection with the infamous murder case. The man was an acquaintance of Lillian's relatives in Cleveland. When she visited them, he begged to be introduced to her. She and her husband raised a large family and lived long, happy lives.

Rosslyn Ferrell was buried in Union Cemetery. His parents spared no expense on his fine monument.

CHAPTER 3

MADAM JENNIE GOOD

S ex, like candy, is addictive—the more you have, the more you want. Men will pay well for great sex. One woman, Steubenville madam Jennie Good, took great advantage of that fact. Catherine Jane "Jennie" Good was born in Morgantown, West Virginia, to a candy store owner and his wife. But don't let her humble beginnings fool you—she didn't grow up to be America's sweetheart! The fiery wildcat and her mother, Sarah, headed to Steubenville around 1884, after the death of Jennie's father. Bound and determined to make it in the bustling town, they turned to a life of prostitution. Jennie's earliest recorded arrest was on April 3, 1886, when she violated section 85 of the codified ordinances of the city of Steubenville. That was the violation for keeping of a house of ill fame, for which the young madam was fined fifteen dollars. Section 85 would be her favorite violation for years to come. Her mother, Sarah, known as Sadie, passed away in 1891 but not before racking up a few Section 85 violations for herself.

Jennie's business ventures included a saloon on Market Street and operating a resort on Water Street. She purchased the Park House, preceding William Horner as the owner. On February 14, 1890, after the state conducted a series of raids on illicit houses in Steubenville, fourteen indictments were handed down. Among them, William and Barbara Horner, of the Ohio Valley House, and Jennie Good of the Park House were each handed two indictments and sent to the Canton workhouse. Jailbirds of a feather flock together.

In January 1896, Jennie was sent the workhouse again on the same charge. After getting out, she married her bartender, George "Dode" Mackinaw, a local hood. A few months into the couple's tumultuous marriage, Jennie caught him in a house on South Street with another prostitute. She woke up the neighborhood with an extremely unladylike catfight. The commotion caught the attention of Officer Lafayette Mercer. The Steubenville police officer carted the still-clawing kitty off to the city jail.

By August 1897, Jennie was the proprietor of the Ohio Valley House. On August 30, the Water Street houses were raided again. Jennie and a male companion fled to Wheeling to avoid prosecution. Dode Mackinaw fled too, taking some of Jennie's jewelry with him. The pair hunted Mackinaw down. They finally found him in a Benwood whorehouse. Her companion took Mackinaw outside and settled the score with him. Mackinaw disappeared for a while after that, and his family feared the worst. However, he turned up alive and well a few months later. In April 1898, Jennie grew tired of being on the run and gave herself up to the Steubenville police. She paid a $150 fine and was sent to the workhouse for ninety days.

Charges of running a house and selling illegal alcohol were leveled against Jennie again in October 1899. Once again, she fled to Wheeling, where it was rumored she was in the hospital. A couple weeks later, she came back to Steubenville and was accused by one of her girls, Cora Welch, of assault and battery and keeping a house of prostitution. The charges stemmed from the night of November 14, when Cora refused to obey Jennie's house rules. The iron-fisted madam beat her about the head and face in a wild rage. Two of Cora's teeth were knocked loose, and her lip was badly cut. True to Jennie's character, she fled to Wheeling with a male companion. After her return to Steubenville, she was placed under arrest and fined sixty dollars.

By 1900, Jennie and Dode Mackinaw divorced and went their separate ways, though their seedy paths often crossed in the brothel mecca along Water Street.

Later in that same year, Jennie married George Ovington, a once-respectable businessman who had fallen under the Madam's spell. George had been married to Mary Emma Gossett, the typhoid-stricken mother of his three children. After divorcing her and leaving his children and ex-wife in the care of his in-laws, he and Jennie were married. Mary Emma died in 1903.

In January 1910, Ovington's children and his ex-in-laws were severely burned when a gas leak caused their home on Washington Street to explode. Fortunately, none of the family lost their lives, but his daughter Jean suffered facial and upper torso burns that would scar her for the rest of her life. George and Jennie took the children with them to Pittsburgh, where Jean could receive expert medical care for her burns. The family lived in

Pennsylvania for a few years before coming back to Steubenville. The couple opened up the Ovington Hotel at 111 North Third Street, where they also resided. George was the bartender and advertised their fine assortment of liquors and wine. It may have been George and Jennie's feeble attempt at a legitimate business, but it's hard to teach an old madam new tricks. The Ovington Hotel was just a fancier version of the Ohio Valley House. Jennie's girls just moved uptown. Unfortunately, for Madam Jennie, her vast arrest record and past displays of public drunkenness kept her under the careful scrutiny of not only the law but also the Anti-Saloon League and Woman's Christian Temperance Union. Uptown was full of churches and law-abiding citizens. They saw to it that the unscrupulous madam was run back to the south end of town. She and George took up residence on South High Street, not far from her Water Street roots.

The passage of the Rose Law in 1908 saw saloons being shut down and the underground speakeasies sprouting up. After passage of the Volstead Act in 1920, life wasn't so good for George and Jennie. The influx of narcotics into Steubenville's underworld had attracted the madam. It was one more way to control her girls, but she had also fallen under their addictive spell. The madam who, over the last thirty years, had been found numerous times passed out drunk by the Panhandle railroad tracks on South Street was now a junkie. She and one of her girls, Foxy Fuller, were busted with narcotics in August 1922. While Jennie paid a fine of $250, Foxy was released upon her promise to leave the city. The whirlwind life of George and Jennie had just reached a new low.

In August 1927, George and Jennie were returning home from visiting friends in Sandusky County, Ohio. Stormy weather had made the roadways treacherously slick. The roadster they were riding in skidded on the wet road. "George, look out!" Jennie screamed as the automobile swerved sharply. George lost control of the careening vehicle, and it overturned, throwing him clear. He suffered a few bruises and scratches. Jennie wasn't so lucky, as the rolling hunk of metal landed on top of her. She died at the scene from a crushed chest and skull.

Buried at Union Cemetery, the once-fiery wildcat rests under one of the most spectacular monuments in the massive graveyard. Ironically, it is the monument of a beautiful angel. She rests next to George, his ex-wife, his former in-laws and one of his daughters. Jennie's brother William, who was blind since birth, also rests in the same plot. It was a complicated family in life, as well as in death. The candy store owner's daughter had a bittersweet life, but she's God's angel now. George Ovington had married four times

Monument depicting the final resting place of Water Street madam Jennie Good. Located in Union Cemetery, Steubenville, Ohio. *Photo by Susan Guy.*

in his life. His third marriage was to Marie Tressler, just a few months after Jennie's death. He and Marie ran a boardinghouse, so to speak. Most of the inhabitants were young women. Marie passed away some years later. In 1943, George married a widow named Daisy Shepherd. They made their home in East Springfield and lived a quiet life. He died there in 1957 and was buried by Jennie in Union Cemetery.

CHAPTER 4

GEORGE MACKINAW

Life after Jennie Good didn't change much for George Mackinaw. He stayed in the spotlight of the law until the very end. Soon after his divorce from the madam of Water Street, he married Elizabeth Stewart, another prostitute, who was pregnant with his child. Their relationship was volatile from the start.

He and several other Steubenville thugs, George Harris and the four Wind brothers, schemed to stay ahead of Ohio's new laws that stiffened the penalties for prostitution, gambling and bootlegging. They decided to buy a riverboat. In the early 1900s, the railroad took over much of the freight hauling business. Shipping by boat was becoming unpopular, and boats were being sold to private individuals. The toughs bought a riverboat in Pittsburgh and revamped it into an illegal moneymaker.

In 1904, the mysterious saloon boat appeared at the bottom of Washington Street. Curious onlookers would stare at it from afar. For weeks, the brightly lit den of debauchery floated in seeming defiance of all that was good. Night after night, loud music and drunken laughter filled the air as Steubenville residents tried to sleep. Concerned, angry citizens complained to the police. The Woman's Christian Temperance Union, which boasted six hundred members, wanted the boat gone. But there was a problem with that. The boat was anchored just off the Ohio shore, within the jurisdiction of West Virginia. Steubenville police and the Jefferson County sheriff couldn't touch it. The Brooke County sheriff just across the river was relieved that he didn't have the partygoers near his shore. He ignored the floating albatross. It looked like the thugs had won this round.

During the midnight hour on July 18, 1904, the sinful partying continued aboard the riverboat. "Is it me, or are we tilting?" Mackinaw asked Ralph Wind. "Naw, you're just drunk!" Wind laughed, as they continued to swill. The boat sank in three feet of water within a few minutes. Screams and curse words filled the air, waking local residents. The silhouettes of twelve men and women could be seen wading to shore, where police were waiting to cart the belligerent bunch off to jail. The Wind brothers, George Harris and George Mackinaw were among the drenched dozen. The cause for the sudden submersion was never mentioned. Could it have been divine intervention? We'll never know.

George and Elizabeth's marriage was as rocky as that sinking boat. When he tried to divorce her for adultery—ironically, with his best friend and partner, George Harris—the judge gave him a severe tongue lashing, saying, "You expect me to grant you a divorce after you've kept an illicit house for years and made your wife work there to provide you an income! You, my dear sir, are very well-known to this court." Judge Richards continued, "You will never be granted a divorce here." With those words, he granted Elizabeth Mackinaw fifteen dollars alimony a month and dismissed the couple from his court. It may be one of the only times in history that a wife was given alimony but not a divorce. The unscrupulous couple were stuck with each other, whether they liked it or not.

George kept to his thug ways and, in 1907, found himself once again in Judge Richards's courtroom. This time, he'd shot a man named Frank Lowe. Richards gave him a five-year stretch in the Ohio Penitentiary.

After serving his time, George came back to Steubenville. He continued his life of crime until death came calling on June 29, 1923. George died at the age of forty-six, of lobar pneumonia. He's buried in Mount Calvary under the stone of an infant child. His relationship to the child is unknown.

CHAPTER 5

THE MURDER OF
PATROLMAN McDONALD

Thirty-nine-year-old John Leslie "Les" McDonald grew up in a complicated household. His father, John McDonald, had been a highly decorated Civil War hero, having served in the First West Virginia Cavalry. He fought at the battle of Gettysburg and also with General George Custer. He was wounded at the Battle of Stevenson's Station, Virginia. Having served since the breakout of the war, John J. McDonald came home at the rank of major. He'd also come home with Bright's disease, which left him sickly. The major was a highly intelligent man, but the ravages of war had hardened him. Not wanting to take up a regular job, he masterminded a scheme with a gang of unscrupulous characters.

They cooked up a con game in which they would find a not-too-bright patsy, who was just as unscrupulous. John would meet the patsy in a hotel room. There, he would reel the guy in by asking him to buy counterfeit money for twenty-five cents on the dollar. Once the money exchanged hands, another member of the gang, pretending to be a marshal, would bust into the room. After confiscating all the money, including the patsy's good money, the so-called marshal would let them go. The scheme worked perfectly for months—until one patsy decided to go to the cops.

An investigation by United States Secret Service and U.S. marshals brought the gang down on July 28, 1874. John J. McDonald, Thomas Martin, George Brown, John Lyons and Jonathan Scarborough were taken to Cleveland, Ohio, and put on trial in federal court. Found guilty, all men were sent to the penitentiary for a long stretch. Lavinia McDonald, a quiet woman, stood by her husband through the trial and sentencing. Once on her own to raise the children, however, she became an independent woman. Cutting ties with her convicted husband, she proceeded to raise a fine family.

This brings the story back to her son, John Leslie "Les" McDonald. He'd worked a number of jobs from bartender to manager of Sohn's store in order to help his mother. But like so many young men, he dreamed of becoming a police officer. His father was a war hero. He couldn't forget that, but neither could he forget being teased at school about the counterfeiting crook. Les could have gone the wrong way easily, if not for his mother's watchful eye. She'd made sure he went to church and stayed out of trouble.

The streets of Steubenville needed more police officers walking the beat. Too many shootings, robberies and drunken brawls infested the streets. After years of mediocre jobs, Les joined the Steubenville Police Department in July 1907. The good-looking, friendly patrolman was a hit with the people on his beat, and he took the job seriously. He worked one of the most dangerous beats in the city, which included Wells Street. During his short career, Les made many arrests and a lot of enemies.

On the day of the Serbian New Year, January 7, 1908, Les reported to work at the station. He'd been ill for a few days, and Mayor Porter told him, "Les, you go home. I'll get another officer to take your place tonight."

Les shrugged it off. "Thanks, Mayor, but I'd rather work. I know the beat and the people better than anybody. I know who the troublemakers are." The mayor reluctantly agreed. At 10:30 p.m., Les met with Officers Haupt, Wilcoxen and Hineman in front of Reddy Kornich's saloon. They laid out a plan to patrol the celebrating crowd in the Serbian section of town near Wells Street and South Fourth. They were looking for drunken shooters, as often happened on Serbian New Year. The officers no sooner went their separate ways than they heard gunshots. Mele Osman, head bartender at Mike Evasovich's saloon, peered out the door. He saw two shadowy male figures talking on the sidewalk a few feet away. Suddenly, he heard gunshots and saw a muzzle flash. Osman watched as one man fled, dropping his hat. The other man fell limp to the ground. The fleeing man ran between the buildings as Osman ran outside. He lit a match and saw the lifeless body of Officer Les McDonald lying in the street. "Oh, my God, it's McDonald!" he cried, as he ran to call Mayor Porter. The officers, who had just left McDonald, returned to see his lifeless body.

Porter arrived with the entire police force just as the ambulance got there. He knelt down to turn the dead officer over. He noticed the sleeve of his overcoat was glowing, evidence of being shot at close range. The faint odor of gunpowder still clung to the night air. Over McDonald's left eye was a gunshot wound, most likely the shot that had killed him. Mayor Porter snuffed out the smoldering sleeve and then noticed that McDonald had also been shot in the stomach. The officer's body was sent to the morgue, as investigators continued to gather evidence. Nearby, they found the officer's gun, with one shot fired. Next to the gun was a strange hat. Osman gave officers a description of the furtive figure who had shot McDonald. "He dropped his hat and then ran between those two houses. I watched him run under the streetlight saw him clearly. I hope you get him," Osman sighed. "Les was a good guy and a friend." Mayor Porter ordered all saloons closed at once, and the manhunt began.

The murder of Steubenville's beloved patrolman set off riots in the downtown. Reddy Kornich bared his chest in front of his saloon, making inflammatory statements about police in his native tongue. When questioned by the mayor, Kornich exclaimed, "I tell my people to help police!" But a bystander, who understood Serbian, told the mayor that the saloon owner was lying. Kornich was saying, "We will kill anyone who bothers us." The angry Serb was arrested, and his boardinghouse/saloon was raided. Inside the establishment, Officer Hineman found Milovan Dodig, the man whose name had come to light as that of the murderer. He blew past Hineman and ran out into Bates Alley, toward Third Street. Officer Charles Haupt, with revolver drawn, met Dodig in the alley and tried to stop him. Dodig wrestled him for the gun until other officers arrived. They overpowered the cop killer, taking him to the ground. He screamed, "Kill me, I no care!" A .38 revolver with two shells spent was found on him. The cops also noticed that Dodig was nursing an injured thumb, courtesy of the round shot off by Les McDonald before he died. The officers escorted Dodig to Mayor Porter's office. As word spread that the murderer of McDonald was in lockup, crowds of angry citizens gathered around the city building. Venturesome Serbs walked toward the lockup, only to be chased back down the block by angry mobs. It was a lively night in Steubenville for one and all.

Milovan Dodig proclaimed his innocence. "I no kill McDonald. A man that I argued with shot me and McDonald." But Mele Osman's eyewitness account stated that Dodig and McDonald were the only two men on the street.

A postmortem examination was done on the body of Les McDonald, and the bullet from his stomach was removed. His mother requested that they leave the bullet lodged in her son's head, as she couldn't bear the thought of them cutting her boy's face up. Citizens of Steubenville filed past the morgue all night, paying their respects to the fallen officer. Though Dodig was a big guy, the six foot, two inch McDonald was a scrappy man and an expert marksman. Many people wondered how Dodig got the drop on him, comparing Les to his father, the heroic West Virginia Calvary soldier.

Dodig was indicted for first-degree murder within seventeen hours of the crime. Patrolman John Leslie McDonald was the first Steubenville police officer ever killed in the line of duty.

Jefferson County prosecutors William Ross Alban and Ernest Finley produced thirty witnesses for the state's case. Cleveland defense attorneys Parsons and Fitzgerald had an equal amount of witnesses. After the jury was seated, a motion brought by the defense to dismiss the case was ignored. Defense's next motion to exhume the body of Officer John Leslie McDonald was brought before Judge Richards. They claimed that the abdominal gunshot was important to their case.

On the morning of March 27, 1908, the body was exhumed from its resting place at Union Cemetery. Sheriff Voorhees accompanied Dr. Floyd and Dr. Elliott to the site, where they were met by a group of thirty Serbians, who wanted to witness the exhumation. Sheriff Voorhees walked over to the group. "You need to leave; only authorized people can be here now," he ordered. The men backed off a few yards but refused to leave. The two doctors erected a white tent, similar to the one that had been erected on that spot for McDonald's funeral a few months earlier. Inside the tent, they built trestles to set the casket on. It was hoisted from the grave and the lid removed. The doctors took the corpse of Les McDonald out, laying it on the rough wooden lid. Even though it had been in the ground for over two months, the body was perfectly preserved, except for some discoloration around the fingertips. The sheriff looked in awe and stated, "Les looks like he's gonna wake up any minute now." A wave of sadness came over him, and he bowed his head as the doctors began their probe.

The abdominal bullet had been extracted by Coroner Campbell on the night of the murder. What was the defense hoping the doctors would find? The bullet over the left eye that had gone through the brain had remained lodged inside McDonald's head. The exhumation was a futile attempt by the defense team and only served to upset McDonald's family, local law enforcement and local citizens.

After a four-day trial, the case was sent to the jury. Jurors deliberated for five hours before coming back with a verdict of guilty of first-degree murder and a recommendation for life without mercy. Judge Richards sentenced Milovan Dodig, a man who couldn't speak or understand English very well, to death by electrocution. The defendant was shaking but showed no other emotions as his interpreter relayed the bad news. He was led to the jail by deputies to await his train ride to the Ohio Penitentiary in Columbus.

In April, while still lodged at the county jail, his attorneys filed a motion for a new trial but were denied.

In August 1908, it was reported in the *Steubenville Herald-Star* that Dodig spent most of his days at the penitentiary reading the Serbian bible. He always had a smile, having accepted his fate.

On December 15, 1908, new defense attorneys Erskine and Smith argued for a new trial for their client, Milovan Dodig. They said, "The State failed to prove premeditation in its case. They couldn't even prove that Dodig and McDonald knew each other before the shooting." E.E. Erskine went on, saying, "When my client made his confession, he was confused and bleeding and surrounded by police officers. The jury was allowed to be impanelled with men who had already made prejudicial statements regarding the case." Erskine finished by saying, "This case was railroaded through court as fast as possible. We demand a new trial."

Grave of murdered Steubenville police officer John Leslie "Les" McDonald. Located in Union Cemetery, Steubenville, Ohio. *Photo by Susan Guy.*

The attorneys got their wish, and a new trial was granted. The end verdict was life with mercy. Dodig was spared the electric chair. He died of tuberculosis while incarcerated at the Ohio Penitentiary.

Les McDonald is buried in Union Cemetery, next to his mother and brothers. His police career had only lasted six months before he paid the ultimate sacrifice, but in that short time, he made a huge difference in many lives. His hero/criminal father is buried with his own mother and siblings in another section of Union Cemetery.

CHAPTER 6

THE WETS AND DRYS
BATTLE IT OUT

The year 1908 was the beginning of a new era in Ohio. The "Wets" and "Drys" had battled for years over the onslaught of saloons that dotted the state like a bad flea infestation on a dog. The Wets wanted their booze and the money that went with it. The Drys fought for a restoration of family values. Those were the sentiments across the nation, and Ohio's November election would be the deciding factor in who won. Isaiah Rose, a junior senator from Marietta, Ohio, had proposed a county-by-county vote for the removal of saloons. His bill was known as the Rose Law. The Anti-Saloon League and Woman's Christian Temperance Union (WCTU) waged a vigorous campaign throughout the state. The Jefferson County chapter of the WCTU boasted six hundred members. Their meetings were held in the Presbyterian Church in Steubenville. Though liquor was only one of the causes women fought for in the early 1900s, it was a major one. These women suffered mentally and physically at the hands of their drunken husbands. Hard-earned money, meant for household bills and food, was being recklessly squandered away.

The WCTU staged parades and protests, wielding signs against liquor establishments and standing outside the doors of saloons. Loud, melodious voices, singing the likes of temperance songs such as "Lips That Touch Liquor Shall Never Touch Mine," floated through the downtown streets, gathering crowds of cheering onlookers. Many saloonkeepers, angered by the spectacle outside their establishments, tried to shoo the protesters away. "Get out of here, or I'll call the police!" many a saloon owner was

Market Street, Water Street and the Jefferson County Courthouse before the Market Street Bridge was built, circa 1900. *Photograph courtesy of the Jefferson County Historical Museum Association.*

heard to say. The singing got even louder, as others joined in, and the rattled businessmen ran back inside. Soon, the "closed" sign appeared in many windows, amid rousing cheers of victory.

These episodes were repeatedly carried out by the WCTU, which scored many a victory. Some saloonkeepers were even persuaded to change professions, closing up shop permanently.

The Wets argued that tax revenue lost due to the breweries and saloons shutting down would be tremendous. Nevertheless, the polls in November showed Jefferson County was one of over forty counties in the state that would go dry. After a thirty-day grace period, the county's 141 saloons and breweries would be closing, and the temperance flag would soon fly over the courthouse. The Wets were astonished at the overwhelming Dry victory. The breweries turned to selling soda pop. Liquor could still be had by prescription for medicinal purposes only.

Months later, the Steubenville council, discouraged by the loss of revenue, wanted to reverse the county ban on liquor. Residents arguing for both sides filled the council chambers. It was determined that council had lost, since the ballots had already been cast in favor of the ban. The city of Steubenville would just have to make do with the revenues they had. Small towns across Ohio were also feeling the pinch. The Rose Law was repealed in 1912.

Though the WCTU and Anti-Saloon League had suffered a setback, they would continue to fight for their cause.

CHAPTER 7

PATROLMAN
LAFAYETTE MERCER

On April 10, 1895, Lafayette Reed Mercer became the first black officer on the Steubenville police force. He walked a rough beat in the south end of town that included the infamous Water Street and many of Steubenville's eighty saloons. Known to his friends as Lafe, he participated in many raids on saloons, stills and illicit houses. He was a good-natured man and enjoyed doing his job. His friends included both black and white officers, with whom he'd go on fishing and camping trips to Brown's Island. Being an avid sportsman, he belonged to one of the local baseball teams.

Lafe had been one of the responding officers to Park House when William Horner murdered his wife, Barbara. He'd run Madam Jennie Good and her mother, Sadie, to lockup on many occasions.

In June 1897, one of the Steubenville night patrol officers had bought a bicycle. He and fellow officers, including Mercer, were learning how to ride it. It wasn't long before most of the night shift had bought their own bicycles and were patrolling their beats on the two-wheeled contraptions. Lafe Mercer had become an expert bicyclist. The Steubenville Police Department thought the wheels were a great idea and hoped that one day they could get their whole department mobile instead of relying on the trolley.

For twenty years, Mercer was the beloved cop on the beat, one of those familiar faces you'd expect to see every day. But things were about to change. On July 2, 1914, officers Smith and McCarty answered a domestic call at the Adams Street home of Albert L. Johnson, a well-known black barber. They were met by a sobbing Mrs. Johnson, sporting a black eye. "Al came

1900 to 1920: Pre-Prohibition Era

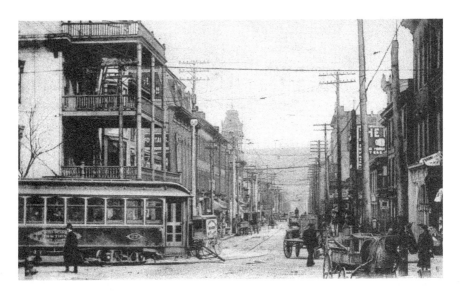

Market Street in 1910. *Postcard from the collection of Susan Guy. Erwin and Robinson of Steubenville, Ohio.*

home drunk and smelling of cheap perfume," she cried. "We quarreled over another woman, Emma Lyons. He's been seeing her for a while. I can't take it anymore!" She continued, "He hit me and then went upstairs." It was learned by the officers that Johnson had left the house to drink at an underground speakeasy, where he had rendezvoused with Ms. Lyons. He returned a few hours later, and the marital spat ensued. That's when Mrs. Johnson made her first complaint to the police, under the mistaken impression that she could have him arrested without a warrant. Smith and McCarty were in the process of telling her to swear out a warrant when Al appeared at the top of the stairway, revolver in hand, saying, "You try to arrest me, and I'll kill you!" The two cops quickly exited the residence, after urging Mrs. Johnson to seek a warrant. She immediately took their advice. A warrant was given to Officer Mercer to serve later that evening, when he went on duty. Lafe told his captain, "Just leave him to me. I'll bring him in."

Arriving at the Johnsons' Adams Street residence, Lafe Mercer was met by Al, who was sitting on his front porch. The two men had known each other for years. "Pull up a chair, Lafe," Al smiled, and with a wave of his hand, pointed to a chair on the porch.

"Don't mind if I do, Al," Lafe chuckled. "Nice night to sit out and enjoy the stars. My poor ole tired feet could use a rest. Walkin' this here beat after all these years is tough on an old body," the officer sighed as he sat down.

They talked for a few minutes and then Lafe pulled out the affidavit that had been sworn out by Al's wife. Johnson leaped from his chair, pulled a revolver from his pants and fired five shots into the warm July night. Two of the shots hit their intended mark. Mercer, wounded twice in the chest, fell backward. Drawing his weapon, the mortally wounded officer fired three shots before dying. The shots struck Johnson in his groin and both legs. The shooting had attracted a crowd of stunned bystanders, many of whom knew both men. One of the wounded barber's stray bullets had struck a man walking a few blocks away. Another stray shot had shattered the window of a business across the street.

Both men were lying on the front lawn when the police and ambulance arrived. Officer Lafayette R. Mercer, the oldest member of the Steubenville Police Department, lay dead. His murderer and longtime friend Albert L. Johnson died nine hours later at the city hospital. Emma Lyons, the so-called other woman, was rounded up and taken to jail for questioning.

At the morgue, Mercer's body underwent an autopsy. Bullets were found lodged in the backbone, having penetrated his lungs.

His funeral was held at the Victoria Theater. The entire Steubenville Police and Fire Departments turned out in full force to show respect for their fellow officer. They laid two large wreaths near the luxurious casket, adorned with banners that said, "Our Brother." Also present at the funeral were the entire Mingo Police Department and members of the Wellsburg and Wheeling Police Departments. Many of Steubenville's most prominent citizens were in attendance. Most notably absent from the large funeral was

Grave of murdered Steubenville police officer Lafayette Reed Mercer. Located in Union Cemetery, Steubenville, Ohio. *Photo by Susan Guy.*

the presence of any black citizens, aside from Mercer's family. It is said that they were upset at the killing of Albert Johnson and chose to stay away, even though Johnson had initiated the fateful gun battle. Lafayette Mercer now rests in the family plot at Union Cemetery in Steubenville.

The heroism of the charismatic officer was undeniable, from all of the crimes he'd helped solve to his run-ins with the thugs on Water Street. Lafayette Reed Mercer was a credit to the Steubenville Police Department to the end. The city of Steubenville had honored him for it with a funeral fit for a king. He was the second city patrolman to be killed in the line of duty.

PART II
NEWSFLASH:
PROHIBITION ARRIVES AND CRIME RATE SOARS

CHAPTER 8

THE ARRIVAL OF PROHIBITION

The "Roaring Twenties" was a wild time in our country's history, with industries popping up everywhere. Automobiles were getting faster and more plentiful, and telephones were making communication instantaneous. The women's movement had won numerous victories, including the right to vote. Life was swirling fast. On January 16, 1919, the passage of the Volstead Act, more popularly known as the Prohibition law, threatened to put a big damper on those wild lifestyles. People weren't going to take it sitting down. Congress passed the law, despite its being vetoed by President Woodrow Wilson. Enacted on January 16, 1920, prohibition of the sale, distribution and manufacture of alcohol produced an unwelcome change in the country, though the consumption of .05 percent alcohol was not illegal. Normally peaceful people turned their frustration at not being able to drink into a hatred for the law. This in turn led to extreme acts of violence against police and federal enforcers of Prohibition, also known as dry agents. Criminals saw a chance to make serious money by supplying the liquor that the public demanded. The mob was already in the business of supplying illegal gambling and prostitution. It now saw a chance to make even more money with bootleg liquor. This was the beginning of organized crime and the gangster period in the United States.

With the laws of Prohibition not being clearly defined, underpaid and undertrained Prohibition agents, operating under the United States Treasury Department, were hired to find stills and raid the underground speakeasies that were sprouting up by the thousands. Many of these dry agents broke

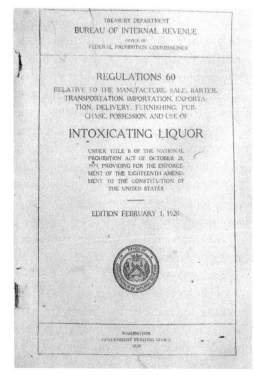

Above: Ohio Prohibition celluloid pin from the 1920s. Made by Bastian Brothers of Rochester, New York. *Photograph by Susan Guy.*

Left: Prohibition Regulations from February 1920, put out by the Bureau of Prohibition. *Public Domain.*

the law or were easily bribed. As a result, many ended up going to prison. These dry agents were often set up by the mob as a way to sully their good reputations with rumors of being on the take. While there were quite a few corrupt dry agents, the un-corruptible ones had to watch their backs every time they stepped out of their homes. Soon, even their homes wouldn't be safe. A large number of dry agents were violently murdered across the United States. In 1922, Jefferson County, Ohio, held the nationwide record for dry agent murders. The federal Prohibition inspector began placing ads in local papers warning Americans about the lengths that criminals would go to ensure that their illegal activities would continue unscathed. Prohibition agents were being offered bribes of up to $300,000 a month to look the other way. In the 1920s, that was a hell of a lot of money. It took men of strong character to turn those bribes down.

CHAPTER 9

THE MIKE VELTRY MURDER

Mama, I be back in a little while. I go for a ride with Dominic and the boys." With that, Mateo "Mike" Veltry gave his wife, Carmen, and their children each a big hug and kiss, grabbed his coat and left their Washington Street home. That would be the last time Carmen would ever see her husband alive. On the evening of Monday, February 28, 1921, the Italian immigrant went to the poolroom owned by fellow Italian Dominic Epifano. Frank Carducci had arrived and joined the two men. Veltry, a local dry agent who worked out of Justice Henry Lawler's court, had fallen into bad graces with Epifano and the others. He had repeatedly arrested them on gambling charges and Prohibition violations. He'd received numerous death threats for the way he operated. He was known to carry large sums of cash in order to negotiate liquor deals and then swoop in for the arrest. Tonight, he would pay the ultimate price for those actions.

At 10:30 a.m. on Tuesday, March 1, 1921, the bloody body of dry agent Mike Veltry was found in a ditch on Sunset Boulevard near Becker Alley. He was found by local coal truck drivers Thomas Beckett and Fred Thomas. The two men were hauling a load of coal from Wintersville when they noticed a pool of blood on the roadway. They pulled off the roadway and got out of their rig, following the blood trail leading to the ditch. To their horror, the body of a man with a bullet-riddled head stared back at them. Sickened by the grisly sight and the overpowering smell of death, they notified Sheriff Ed Lucas. Lucas sent Deputy William Yost to the scene. He was accompanied by acting coroner William Downer. Both men immediately knew the identity of the corpse: Mike Veltry, a man whom they'd worked alongside on many cases.

The body was taken to Lindsay's funeral home for examination. At first, it was surmised that Veltry had died from a crushed skull. After the autopsy, Sheriff Lucas learned that Mike Veltry had been shot five times with a .38 revolver. The deceased dry agent was known to carry a .38, and his wife, Carmen, told Sheriff Lucas that her husband left home with his gun that night. "Mateo went to the poolroom," she sobbed. "He tell me that he be right back."

Lucas paid a visit to Dominic "Jimmy" Epifano at the poolroom. He was aware of the history between the two men. Epifano admitted that he and Frank Carducci had gone for a ride that evening in Epifano's Nash, taking Veltry along, but staunchly denied having anything to do with Veltry's murder. "Mateo was my friend. I would not hurt my friend," he cried. "We shoot pool and then go for a ride." Epifano explained that they had tried driving up Market Street, but his car couldn't make the hill. They turned around in the middle of the hill and drove to a garage, where repairs were made on the car. Around 7:30, they started out once again up Market Street. It was determined that Carducci had not been in the alleged murder car on the second trip. His charges were dropped, and he became a material witness for the state. It was learned that a third passenger was in the car. He was identified as Nick Pellegrino, an Italian fruit dealer. Before his arrest, Nick was in the process of collecting money and flowers for Veltry's widow and children. Pellegrino admitted he had been in the car but denied any knowledge of the shooting. "We go for ride, and then we drop Mateo off on Washington Street," Pellegrino stated, "then we go home."

Sheriff Lucas located Epifano's Nash in his garage on Sumner Alley. It had been partially washed in a poor attempt to get rid of evidence. In their haste, the perpetrators had forgotten to clean blood spatter from the interior roof, and the Nash was minus a windshield. It was located behind a pile of rubbish, shattered and spattered with blood and pieces of skin. From the evidence gathered at the garage, it was surmised that Epifano had been driving, with Mike Veltry in the passenger seat and Pellegrino in the back seat. Veltry's crushed skull resulted from being dragged feet first from the automobile, his head bouncing off the running board onto the brick road.

Lucas made his way back to the jail where Epifano, Pellegrino and Carducci were still incarcerated. Using a magnifying glass, Sheriff Lucas examined Epifano's coat, on which he found several droplets of blood. Confident that he had more than enough evidence against the men, he went to the prosecutor. The defendants waived their rights to a preliminary hearing on the advice of their attorneys. Two weeks later, the case went to the grand jury, which failed to indict the trio. Two subsequent grand juries did the same thing. For some baffling reason, the prosecution failed to introduce the crucial evidence gathered by Sheriff Lucas and his men. One of the coldest, bloodiest murders in Jefferson County history went unavenged. Could fear and intimidation have played a part in this huge failure of the justice system?

Traumatized widow Carmen Veltry fled back to Italy with her daughter. The Veltrys' only son, Anthony, had died a year earlier. Veltry had worked with four other dry agents. One fled to Italy after having his life threatened. Another one, who had been sworn in the same day as Veltry in July 1919, had been lured to Beech Bottom in Brooke County, West Virginia, where he had been brutally murdered a few months earlier. Two other dry agents were also murdered around the same time—one in Washington County, Pennsylvania, and the other in Hancock County, West Virginia.

The three suspects in Veltry's death went on with their lives as though nothing had happened. Dominic Epifano lived a long life with his wife and children. He died a natural death in 1971. Frank Carducci married and had a family but died at the age of forty in 1935. His cause of death was cirrhosis of the liver, brought on by his bootleg liquor. Nick Pellegrino died on January 8, 1927. His story will be told later.

Mateo "Mike" Veltry is buried in an unmarked grave in Union Cemetery. Like a scene from *The Untouchables*, his was a true gangland-style murder and helped to set the tone in Steubenville as the "Little Chicago" of the country. Gangland shootings would become the norm in Jefferson County.

CHAPTER 10

THE FRANK PERRIN MURDER

As the gangland murders were heating up in Steubenville, dry agents were becoming an increasing threat to bootleggers, interfering with their highly profitable business ventures in the never-ending demand for illegal alcohol. Local and federal dry agents faced insurmountable odds, with little training or backing by city and county officials. Friends turned on friends, and trust was a thing of the past. Unlike the infamous Prohibition crime fighter Eliot Ness and his "Untouchables," who were busy battling gangster Al Capone and his mob of bootleggers in Chicago, Jefferson County dry agents were brutally getting touched.

Frank Perrin (or Peron) was one of those unfortunate dry agents. On February 19, 1922, Perrin's bullet-riddled body was found on the road between Piney Fork and Newell in Jefferson County. One year earlier, the body of another murdered dry agent, Mike Veltry, had been discovered. Perrin, a married Newell mine owner, had been shot four times at close range. All four shots struck him in the mouth. It was an execution-style killing that had been seen many times before in the country in recent years. Local residents were startled by the rapid-fire shots at around 6:30 p.m. An hour later, several men came upon Perrin's body lying in the middle of the road. The sheriff and coroner weren't notified of the murder until the next morning.

The thirty-five-year-old dry agent had served under Marshal John Cole of Smithfield. His life had been threatened openly many times. The threats came from a loud bunch of Piney Fork boys with whom he and Cole had multiple run-ins. Perrin had been traveling to one of his mines when he was ambushed. Sheriff Ed Lucas believed that more than one man was involved in the horrific crime. In an interview with the *Steubenville Herald-Star*, the county's local newspaper, Lucas related that several weeks earlier, he and his men had raided a speakeasy belonging to one of at least four known Piney Fork gangs. While there, they confiscated a bushel basket full of daggers and automatic weapons. "I am confident that one of these gangs is responsible for the murder of Perrin and will be caught," Lucas promised. The straight-as-an-arrow Jefferson County sheriff was bound and determined to apprehend these killers and see to it that justice was done. He wanted to clean up the crime in Jefferson County.

Eyewitness testimonies started to come in the next day. Four persons reported seeing Joe Russo, twenty-three, and another man in the vicinity of the shooting just after it happened. It was Russo's speakeasy that had been raided, and he had been arrested by Frank Perrin recently. Sheriff Lucas drove out to Piney Fork and brought the gangster to the county jail. He expected to have Russo's accomplice behind bars soon. Any member of the gang would've gladly pulled the trigger on Perrin.

It was rumored that Perrin had retired as a dry agent. Those reports were soon discovered to be false when authorities found four arrest warrants in the deceased man's pocket. The other man seen with Joe Russo in the vicinity of Perrin's murder was arrested a few days later. His name was Joe Pergillini. The grand jury failed to indict either of the men due to lack of evidence.

In 1929, Joe Russo was shot and killed by a friend during a drunken brawl. The murder case of Frank Perrin went unsolved, just like the case of Mike Veltry. Perrin is buried at Georgetown Cemetery on State Route 250, near Adena, in an unmarked grave. The Italian immigrant left his widow and a son and daughter.

CHAPTER 11

THE MURDER OF
HICKS CUMMINS

Thirty-three-year-old Harry Dean Cummins, known as "Hicks" to everybody in Steubenville, was a handsome, likeable young man. He was a World War I army veteran who had repaired heavy equipment and vehicles over in France during his time in the military. That knowledge served him well when he came back to the United States. The former Bell Telephone operator opened up a Ford dealership and garage with his father, Harry W. Cummins, on Court Street. Their business grew quite large, and Hicks was a familiar face and popular young man around Steubenville.

On the morning of July 23, 1923, a stranger came into the dealership. Hicks crawled out from under a car he was working on and greeted the customer. He said, "Hello, sir. May I help you?"

"Yes, my name's McDowell," the man replied. "I was interested in taking that Ford over there for a demonstration." He gestured to one of the older Fords in the garage.

"Can you come back about 12:30?" Hicks asked. "I need to finish this car up, and then I'll be able to take you for that demonstration ride."

"I'll be back then," McDowell answered. The two men shook hands, and McDowell left. Hicks's father was sweeping out the garage and took note of the verbal exchange. Clare Cummins, Hick's sister and secretary for the garage business, had stepped out of the office to speak to her father. She nodded to McDowell and then walked over to her father to discuss a business matter.

At 12:30, the stranger returned to the Cummins Garage, and the two men jumped in the old Ford touring car and drove up Market Street. Hicks waved

Harry Dean "Hicks" Cummins. *Photograph courtesy of the* Steubenville Herald-Star. *Used with permission.*

to a lot of people he knew as they traveled along Sunset Boulevard, turning onto Lover's Lane. The demonstration rides were a daily routine for Hicks, and it wasn't unusual to see the jovial salesman taking a customer for a spin.

Back at the garage, closing time came, and Hicks hadn't returned with McDowell or the Ford. H.W. went home, fuming that Hicks hadn't returned to help him close the business up for the evening. The next morning, H.W. came downstairs for breakfast. Clare informed him that Hicks hadn't come home. "Father, Hicks's bed wasn't slept in last night," she said, "I'm worried."

"Something's not right," H.W. agreed, shaking his head. "That's not like Hicks at all."

The concerned father called the police and told them that Hicks had disappeared after taking this McDowell for a drive in one of their used Fords. Steubenville police chief Blaine Carter and Jefferson County sheriff Ed Lucas orchestrated a manhunt for Hicks Cummins and the car he had last been seen in. The Jefferson County commissioners offered a $500 reward for information concerning Hicks's whereabouts. Boy Scout troops searched, along with hundreds of townspeople, looking for any sign of what may have happened to the popular young mechanic. For two days, the manhunt continued—until word was received by the sheriff that Hicks had been found.

At about 1:00 p.m. on July 25, Charles Richardson and Ernest Hurl were out searching for some lost cattle on Permar's Run, when they noticed a rank odor coming from the direction of the creek. When they looked over the embankment, both men saw the decomposing body of Harry "Hicks" Cummins, with his head smashed in. Sadly, his body was found less than half a mile from the Cumminses' home.

A mob mentality grew in Steubenville, as people agonized over who could have possibly perpetrated such a horrible crime on the handsome young garage owner and beloved war veteran. An autopsy revealed that Hicks had been shot in the temple, and the bullet lodged in his brain. The coroner's findings also revealed that a vicious blow from the butt of a .32-caliber revolver used in the crime had caused the head's mashed-in appearance. The blow to Cummins's head was so forceful that nobody realized he had been shot until the autopsy had been performed. Numerous scratches on the victim's arms indicated that Hicks had put up a valiant fight for his life. A search for the murder car was still ongoing as witnesses started coming forward. An eyewitness who had seen Hicks and his passenger drive by identified the alleged perpetrator, known as McDowell. His real name was Howard Mitchell, alias Harry Carman, a barber from Wellsville. The manhunt turned its attention toward the Columbiana County town, just north of Steubenville, in search of the fugitive barber. Chief Carter learned that Howard Mitchell had just married a young Wellsville girl, Rosalie Watters, on July 6. Mitchell used an alias because he was already married to a woman in Fort Wayne, Indiana, and was wanted there for nonsupport and bigamy.

Mingo Junction resident Albert Helmbright was en route to a Steubenville garage when his automobile was struck by a Ford touring car at 2:30 p.m. on the day of the murder at the intersection of Prospect Avenue and Steubenville-Mingo Boulevard. The front tire of the murder car had been torn off in the collision, and Mr. Helmbright's fender had been damaged. The Ford driver had Helmbright take him to Kincaid's Garage on Third Street, where the man promised to pay for repairs to both vehicles.

Rumors had been circulating for a few days that five men had been involved in the horrific murder. Those rumors were put to rest when Chief Joe Morrow at the La Belle Iron Works notified Sheriff Lucas that a couple of foreigners who worked at the mill had related a story from the day of the murder to him. He brought the two men to Sheriff Lucas, and they repeated their story to him. On the day of the murder, they had been stopped by a gentleman fitting Mitchell's description on Permar's Run. He told them that he couldn't get his vehicle started, so they assisted him, and the men rode on the running boards with him to a gasoline station at the corner of South and Third Street. The sheriff took the two men back out to Permar's Run to reenact the meeting with Mitchell. They explained that they had been out picking berries with another man and his son and noticed the car parked on the side of the road. A man suddenly stepped from behind a clump of bushes and told them that his car wouldn't start. They offered to help, just as farmer Robert Dailey and his daughter passed by in their buggy. The man told the foreigners that he was en route to Bridgeport. A short time later, upon taking the men back to Permar's Run, the Ford was involved in the accident with Albert Helmbright.

Armed with this new information, authorities revisited the theory that only one man had committed the murder. Meanwhile, at East Liverpool, justice of the peace Scott Rowan knocked on the door of Mitchell's residence and was greeted by wife number two, Rosalie. After some prodding, she reluctantly gave him a recent photograph of her husband and told Rowan that her husband was in Cleveland. She stated that he had been there for a few weeks and couldn't possibly have had anything to do with the murder.

On Monday, August 1, 1921, Rowan arrested Mitchell in Cleveland, at Winan's Hotel, in the barbershop. Rosalie had accompanied Rowan to Cleveland. Upon hearing of the arrest, Sheriff Lucas and Prosecutor Enoch Stanton Pearce met the train at the station in Salem, where they greeted Mr. and Mrs. Howard Mitchell as they stepped from the train. Mitchell was taken straight to the Columbiana County jail at Lisbon. He vehemently denied having anything to do with the crime and stated that he had over one hundred witnesses who would swear that he was working at the Cleveland barber shop, where he was currently employed. He had not been in Steubenville since July 11. Sheriff Lucas decided to keep Mitchell in the Columbiana County jail, due to the fact that it might be safer for him. The next day, Steubenville eyewitnesses came, one by one, to the jail to identify the alleged murderer. To Lucas's dismay and surprise, H.W. Cummins; his daughter, Clare; and Albert Helmbright, along with the foreigners, stated that Mitchell was not the same man they saw on the day of the murder. Walter Kincaid, the owner of Kincaid's garage where the murder car was found, also denied that Mitchell was the man who had brought the car in for repairs.

It had been learned that the killer had stayed at Fleet Walker's hotel. Authorities searched the room and also learned that he spent time in the company of Foxy Fuller, a prostitute who was well known to police. Foxy was taken to jail as a potential witness, but she couldn't add much to what police already knew.

Deputy Sheriff William Campbell made a trip to Cleveland to check up on Mitchell's alibi. He had been employed at the Winan Hotel's barbershop and was there from July 20 until the time police picked him up. Over a dozen reliable witnesses gave written statements to Deputy Campbell. Steubenville barber John Hart was in Cleveland on the day of the murder, visiting Mitchell, and gave a written statement to that fact. On August 3, Mitchell was set free, and law enforcement officials were back at square one.

On Tuesday, August 9, at about 3:00 a.m., a gentleman named Abe Long notified the Wellsville police that his automobile had been stolen. From the description, Chief J.H. Fulz recognized the car thief as Wallace, aka Walter Wright. Chief Fulz went to the residence of Wright's father, who told him that Walter had joined a road show called Stanton-Huntington Players. It was a wagon show that was currently playing in Maynard, down in Belmont County. Fulz, along with officers Finch and Priest, went to Belmont County in search of the stolen vehicle. The description of Wright also fit the description of the man wanted in connection with the Cummins murder. All three men knew in their guts that their suspect was one and the same. The officers arrived in St. Clairsville and began showing townspeople a photograph of Walter Wright. They spent the greater part of the day tracking down leads, but to no avail.

En route back to Columbiana County, the officers spied a Ford touring car parked on the roadside, just east of the St. Clairsville city limits. It was pointed west, and it had no front license plate. The officers pulled up to the front of the car and approached it with caution. In the back seat, Walter Wright was sound asleep, with a .32-caliber revolver lying next to him. Finch carefully opened the door. Wright woke up, and a brief struggle ensued. The revolver was knocked to the floor and was quickly secured by another officer. On August 11, the wanted man was finally in custody. An accomplice named Joe Doyle was taken into custody in Martins Ferry, having been with Wright when they stole the Long automobile. Doyle had gone to police when he learned of the murder, figuring out that Wright must have been the shooter.

The owner of the Stanton-Huntington players told authorities that he had loaned Wright his revolver when Wright wanted to return to Wellsville to see his family. It was also learned that Wright had escaped from an Ohio prison, having served two sentences there—one for murder and another for criminal assault.

At 3:00 p.m. that afternoon, Walter Wright broke down in the county jail and blurted out, "I killed him because I wanted the automobile." With that, the twenty-eight-year-old self-confessed murderer made a complete statement to the police regarding the murder of Harry Dean "Hicks" Cummins. The confession was made after H.W. and Clare Cummins positively identified Wright as the man they saw in their garage, negotiating a deal for the Ford with Hicks on the day of the murder. Before they had identified him as the culprit, Wright had lied to Chief Carter, saying he was just passing through Steubenville and had never stopped in the city.

During the interrogation, Wright told of the fateful ride on July 23 that led to Hicks Cummins's death. Hicks had told Wright, aka McDowell, that day that they would drive out to Lover's Lane, then down Permar's Run and back into the city. Once they got to Permar's Run, Wright asked Hicks to pull over. After the car stopped, Wright got out and walked over to a field by the side of the road and climbed the fence. Hicks allegedly followed him. That was the moment when Wright decided to take the car. He turned and shot Hicks in the head, claiming there was no struggle at all. The victim tried to get up on his feet and staggered. That's when Wright pushed him over the hill and into the creek bed. Never having driven before, he was trying to start the Ford touring car when the four foreigners came by and offered to assist him.

After making his confession, Wright stared at the roomful of police officers and newspaper reporters, who sat in stunned, wide-eyed silence. How could someone commit such a horrific crime for the theft of an automobile? He read it on their faces, and the reality of what he'd done must have set in, for Wright began to cry. He was taken back to his cell.

The September grand jury indicted Walter Wright for the first-degree murder of Harry Dean "Hicks" Cummins. His trial began on Thursday, October 27, 1921. His defense would be mental irresponsibility, as stated by his attorney, Blaine Cochran. Cochran told the jury that his client, Walter Wright, had

Walter Wright, the killer of Hicks Cummins, died in the electric chair. *Photograph courtesy of Ohio DRC website. Public Domain.*

been unstable since childhood. Prosecutor E. Stanton Pearce would try to prove that the crime was premeditated for the sole purpose of robbery and the defendant knew exactly what he was going to do and when he was going to do it. At 9:00 a.m., Prosecutor Pearce made a motion to have the jurors visit the crime scene. After no objection was raised by the defense, they were taken to the Cummins Garage on North Court Street where the meeting of victim and killer took place. The caravan of jurors then followed the route of the murder car up Market Street to Lover's Lane and then down Permar's Run. Stopping at the sight of the murder, jurors could imagine for themselves what happened on July 23, as Hicks Cummins was shot to death and hurled over the embankment. Several hundred onlookers gathered on Permar's Run to watch the proceedings, as hundreds more waited patiently back at the courthouse for the trial to resume. During the two-and-a-half-hour crime scene outing, Walter Wright appeared to be having a good time, smiling and laughing. His odd behavior was unnerving to those who observed it. Was it an act, or was it just the behavior of a true psychopath?

As the weeklong trial progressed, many witnesses gave damaging testimony regarding the defendant. None, however, would be as damaging as the defendant's own testimony. On October 31, 1921, Walter Wright took the witness stand and underwent a three-hour cross-examination. The *Steubenville Herald-Star* reported that he was "cool as an iceberg" and showed little emotion until he calmly related how he killed Hicks Cummins, without giving the handsome young World War I veteran a chance. Lavinia Hughes, Hicks's fiancée, had been listening to Wright babble on until she couldn't take it anymore. "Why are you wasting time on this murderer?" she cried out, as the crowded courtroom fell dead silent. For a moment, the defendant wavered, and a slight flicker of emotion shone in his eyes. Deputies took Lavinia by the arm and escorted her to a seat, trying to calm down the distraught woman. Wright went on to recite his horrid version of the crime. This time, he made a few adjustments to his story by saying, "I told Cummins that I wanted the car but didn't have any money. Then I was going to force him to sign the papers over to me." He went on, "Cummins got mad and lunged at me, and that's when I shot him in the head." The spectators in the overcrowded courtroom started showing their anger with Wright, and people standing in the aisles started pushing their way forward into the attorneys' area. Judge Smith called for a recess while the deputies cleared the aisles and restored order in the courtroom.

The trial resumed with more witnesses and lasted another day before going to the jury, which didn't take long to find the defendant guilty. Though

Harry "Hicks" Cummins's grave site. Located in Union Cemetery, Steubenville, Ohio. *Photo by Susan Guy.*

his mother fought a long, hard battle to keep her son from the electric chair, Judge Smith sentenced Walter Wright to die by electrocution.

At 12:29 a.m., on March 2, 1922, Walter Wright calmly sat down in Ohio's electric chair and said good-bye to his family and friends. He smiled as his last words were spoken: "Good-bye, Mother." He was dead. Wright was part of a double electrocution as murderer Harry Bland, of Pomeroy, was executed at the same time.

Harry Dean "Hicks" Cummins is buried at Union Cemetery in Steubenville, alongside his parents and sister. His was just one of many young, brilliant lives snuffed out too soon on the streets of Steubenville in the Roaring Twenties.

CHAPTER 12
A WEEK OF MURDER

Forty-two-year-old Edward Still and his wife, Elizabeth Woodward, had been married for fifteen years. Their marriage, by all accounts, was a happy one until 1920. On a chilly October morning, they had a huge fight over marital obligations, after Elizabeth had stayed out all night. Emotions ran high, and their wedded bliss was gone.

In early 1921, Edward went out west with cousins Vern and Bill Martin and his brother and sister-in-law, Willard and Edith Still. They were going to Oregon to work in a logging camp on homestead lands. At that time, cowboy movies were becoming popular, and the merry group of cousins saddled up their horses and lived out their cowboy dreams. Back home on Wills Creek, Elizabeth began seeing other men and wrote to Edward that she was divorcing him. In April 1921, with their divorce final, Elizabeth went back to using her maiden name. This action greatly upset Edward. The wannabe cowboy returned home in August to try and win his beautiful Lizzie back.

The hardworking Edward had been employed by Leamon Martin at Martin Brothers Ice on Wills Creek and had also engineered the roller coaster at Stanton Park before going west. The highly respected man of Alikanna was becoming derailed at the thought of his ex-wife with other men. On the evening of August 20, 1921, he went to Lizzie's Alikanna home, where she was entertaining William S. Dunlavey, a married man with seven children.

Shots from multiple guns were fired through the front door, resulting in one murder victim. Lizzie, with one shot to the stomach and one to the neck, lay dead on the parlor floor. Edward Still had a bullet wound to the left hand. Attracted by the commotion and gunfire, neighbors began gathering on the front lawn. One of them summoned the authorities.

Two stories began to emerge from the incident. According to William Dunlavey, Edward had come to call on Lizzie and became enraged when she wouldn't let him in the door. He allegedly fired through the door, striking her in the stomach. She exclaimed, "Oh, Edward, you shot me!" Then she walked to her bedroom, returning with a revolver. She allegedly returned fire through the front door, hitting Edward in the left hand. He cried, "Oh, Lizzie, you shot me too!" Mr. Dunlavey continued, "I hid under the parlor table and began shooting with my rusty old gun. The bullets were flying wild."

Dr. Montgomery arrived, having been summoned by a next-door neighbor. He met Edward, who was still holding his revolver. Relieving Edward of the weapon, he continued into the house. Edward saw Hugh Martin and his wife standing on the lawn and explained what had happened. Hugh spoke sharply to him, "You had no business going to that house. This is your fault!" The Martins quickly returned to their home. A wounded Edward hung his head and started walking toward his car.

Doc Montgomery turned his attention to Lizzie. She had been shot through the jugular and bled out. Nothing more could be done for her. After gathering up the other two revolvers, he made his way back to Edward, intending to clean and bandage his wound. Edward had swallowed some strychnine tablets and was fading into unconsciousness. Montgomery put Still in his automobile as the sheriff arrived to begin his investigation. He rushed to Gill Hospital, where the dejected man was put on the operating table at 11:00 p.m. Though it was touch-and-go for a while, Still made it through the night but was in great pain. The forlorn widower made a full recovery in time to stand trial.

He was indicted by the grand jury and stood trial on June 22, 1922. During the week that he shot Lizzie, three other murders had occurred in Steubenville. He was incarcerated at the county lockup with eight other alleged murderers who were awaiting trial.

The Still jury consisted of four women and eight men. At 11:00 a.m., the jury was taken to the Woodward home on Wills Creek to view the scene of the murder. Trial began in the afternoon court session with an opening statement by prosecutor Stone, who told the packed courtroom that Still paid an unannounced visit to his ex-wife on Sunday, August 21, 1921. "He became enraged when he saw that she was entertaining Mr. Dunlavey. She urged Still to leave from the doorway and then shut the door in his face," the prosecutor stated. "That's when he fired the first shot." The attorney told the jurors the same story that Dunlavey related to authorities on the night of the murder.

Defense attorneys Cohen and Rogers's opening statements told a totally different version of the fateful night. The divorced couple had talked earlier in the day about financial matters that Edward was going to help her with. They had agreed that Edward would come over on the night of August 21 to talk the matter over. Cohen stated to the jury that Lizzie came out of the house, and she and Edward walked arm in arm, together up and down the lane. For an hour, they talked about getting remarried in September. Returning to the house, they lingered by the gate for a while, before Lizzie opened the door and stepped inside.

While still continuing their conversation in the doorway, Edward spied William Dunlavey, standing behind an inner door, holding a gun down at his side. Attorney Cohen related the conversation to an attentive courtroom audience.

> Dunlavey yelled, "That's right, I've got a gun, and if you don't get out of here right now, I'll use it on you!" With those words, he fired, striking Edward in the left hand. Edward returned fire. As bullets flew wild, Lizzie was struck in the arm at an angle; and the bullet lodged in her stomach. "Edward, I'm shot!" she cried. "Lizzie, I didn't hit you, did I?" Edward gasped, then told her, "I'm hit, too, Lizzie. I'll go call for the doctor." As she disappeared into the house, Edward heard two more shots.

His attorneys put Edward on the stand, and for three hours, he relayed a very convincing and detailed version of the events, culminating with the fact that he didn't know Lizzie had been shot a second time until he woke up in the hospital the next day after his failed suicide attempt.

After two days of witness testimony, including from brothers Hugh and Albert Martin, their wives and other neighbors of the Stills, the case went to the jury on June 24. After the jury deliberated for fifty-five minutes, the defendant was acquitted of second-degree murder on the first ballot. Edward Still was a free man. He died of natural causes in 1963 and is buried in Toronto Union Cemetery.

On August 31, 1922, one year after the murder of Elizabeth Woodward Still and eight weeks after Edward Still was acquitted, Clarence Woodward beat his own wife, trying to strangle her with his bare hands. He had become distraught over his sister Elizabeth's murder. After the trial, his anger increased over her killer's acquittal, and he took it out on his family. His seventeen-year-old son, Herbert, repeatedly screamed for his father to stop, but his pleas fell on deaf ears. With his mother almost dead from lack of oxygen, Herbert grabbed a gun leaning in a corner of the kitchen and fired it at his father. The bullet went through Woodward's shoulder, traveling downward, and lodged near his heart. Within ten minutes, Clarence Woodward was dead in his Knoxville home. After notifying authorities, Herbert was taken to the county jail and held pending investigation into the incident. The sheriff learned that Woodward had taken a razor to his wife's throat the week before. May Woodward went to the prosecutor after that incident to ask for legal advice. She had explained her husband's violent episodes over the recent months. Apparently, the prosecutor's answer hadn't helped family matters. The investigation of Clarence Woodward's death concluded with a self-defense ruling, and Hebert was released from jail.

A number of other murders happened around Jefferson County at the same time that the Wright and Still cases were in the public eye. Jefferson County had a record year for homicides in 1921.

On August 19, 1921, Minnie Fuller, a thirty-seven-year-old married waitress was working her usual evening shift. Her boss, Mrs. Jones, really liked Minnie. She was good with the customers, always greeting them with a cheery smile and her delightful personality. Many of the patrons knew of her illicit affair with Sam Ingle, a married C&P Railroad conductor. They had been seeing each other for a couple years. Minnie's two daughters were living with her estranged husband in Wellsville. She had visited with them earlier that afternoon. Sam had been threatening her over the last few weeks. She told him that she and her husband were going to reconcile for the girls' sake. This revelation didn't set well with Ingle, who had just divorced his wife over the pact that he and Minnie had made to love only each other for the rest of their lives.

The door to the restaurant opened around 6:45 that evening, and Sam Ingle walked in. Mrs. Jones was aware of Minnie's estrangement from Ingle and was, therefore, surprised when Minnie voluntarily walked over to wait on him. "Hi, Sam. Can I get you a cup of coffee?" she grinned cheerfully, setting a glass of water on the lunch counter in front of him. He leaned toward her and, without a word, pulled a .32-caliber revolver from his pocket and fired directly at her face. As she turned to run, the bullet struck her in the back of the neck. He fired three more times as she screamed for help. Two of the bullets struck her in the back and the left upper thigh. She collapsed on the restaurant floor as terrified customers ducked for cover. Ingle tried to make his way out of the restaurant but was tackled by patrons. Patrolmen Hawkins and McCarthy were standing on Market Street, a few doors away, and heard the gunfire. They arrived on the scene and were greeted by three men holding Ingle down. Hawkins placed Ingle under arrest and smelled the heavy odor of alcohol on his breath. They called an ambulance for the victim, but she died before reaching Gill Hospital. On the way to the city lockup, Ingle repeatedly ranted to Hawkins and McCarthy, "I was good to her, and she didn't treat me right."

When Minnie's estranged husband Frank Fuller was called to pick up her remains, the man refused to do so. "She abandoned me and my two girls to run off with that guy. I don't want nothin' to do with her. You bury her," he stated coldly.

After a night's sleep in the jail, Sam Ingle sobered up and was informed by police of Minnie's death. His memory, clouded by booze, had blocked out the previous day's events. He broke down and sobbed uncontrollably, pleading with Sheriff Ed Lucas to let him go see Minnie at the morgue. Sheriff Lucas shook his head, "No, Sam. You said your final good-bye to her yesterday when you killed her." Lucas walked out as the sobbing killer looked down at the floor.

On Saturday, November 7, 1921, Ingle's first-degree murder trial was supposed to begin, but he surprised the packed courtroom when he asked to change his plea. After being advised by the judge of his rights, Ingle pled guilty to the murder charge and threw himself on the mercy of the court. He received a sentence of life in prison. He and Walter Wright, the killer of Hicks Cummins, rode to the penitentiary together, where Ingle died in 1943.

Another murder case that happened around the same time was that of Mike Ollum. On August 14, Ollum was walking along the Ohio River bank at Tiltonsville, which is located at the southern end of Jefferson County, between Rayland and Yorkville. As eyewitness Steven Bartok was looking out his living room window, he saw Ollum taking his usual evening stroll. A man walked toward him, carrying a shotgun in one arm and a couple oars in the other. As the stranger approached Ollum, who seemed oblivious of the man, he dropped the oars, and raised the shotgun. Hearing the oars clatter to the ground, Mike Ollum looked up at the barrel pointed at his face from about twenty feet away. Frozen with fear, he stared at the unknown assailant, who fired the weapon. Ollum fell dead as his assailant was tackled to the ground by three other witnesses and held for authorities. Sheriff Lucas arrived in Tiltonsville to take custody of the murderer, John Scheighter. He was jailed after the investigation, adding one more to the growing list of alleged killers awaiting trial in Jefferson County.

At his trial on December 8, 1921, it was learned that Schleighter had first targeted the Tiltonsville home of Joe Gurilla, who had been playing with his little girl in the front yard. Schleighter approached him and raised the shotgun, but Gurilla scooped his daughter up in his arms and ran around the back of the house. Schleighter did not follow him but instead turned his attention to Ollum.

The Schleighter trial would go down in Jefferson County history as the first time women would be allowed to serve on a jury in a first-degree murder trial. Before the criminal trial even started, Anna Ollum, widow of the murder victim, filed a $5,000 civil lawsuit against John Schleighter for taking her husband's life and depriving her and her minor child of a father and husband. Defense attorneys would claim that their client shot in self-defense to protect himself from an attack by Ollum. Their strategy didn't work, and Schleighter was sentenced to life without parole.

Sheriff Ed Lucas and his men were rounding up murderers as quickly as they could, but getting indictments or guilty verdicts out of the juries was another matter entirely. This would prove true in the case of Rosario "Rosey" Sacco, who murdered Pete Urbano in Gould's Station on October 23, 1921, at the Sacco residence. Sacco and his wife, Emma, had returned home from a visit to Steubenville that evening. They were in their home for just a few minutes when neighbors heard someone yelling for help. When they rushed next door to see what was wrong, they found Pete Urbano on the floor, bleeding from knife and gunshot wounds. He was rushed to Gill Hospital and died a half hour later. Rosey Sacco had disappeared.

Sheriff Lucas learned upon interrogating Emma that the quarrel was over Urbano paying too much attention to her. She had recently filed for divorce from Rosey. Lucas took Emma to jail in hopes that it would bring her husband out of hiding.

On Thursday, October 27, acting on a tip that they'd received, the sheriff and his deputies arrested Rosario Sacco at 9:00 a.m., just west of Gould's Tunnel, where he had been hiding out. Upon his arrest, Emma Sacco was released. He was indicted by the grand jury on first-degree murder.

On June 12, 1922, Rosey's trial went to the jury. They deliberated for four hours and returned with a verdict of guilty of assault and battery. Most jurors, it turns out, believed Sacco's story of self-defense. Since they couldn't reach a unanimous verdict any other way, they figured assault and battery was better than nothing at all. "After all," the jury foreman stated, "Urbano was a killer and was connected to other murders in the county. He got what he deserved."

Emma Sacco divorced Rosey. She would later be brought up on charges and plead guilty to forging postal money orders. She served six months in the county lockup in April 1922. In still another case, she was suspected of stealing jewelry from a man and woman living in the apartment above her. There was no proof of her guilt in that case, and it was dropped. She and her estranged husband ended up remarrying after serving their sentences. They moved to Pennsylvania, where Rosario Sacco worked as a coal miner. Was it a happily ever after story? I doubt it.

CHAPTER 13

THE DIXIE BLINN
MURDER

The rum battles continued in Jefferson County. Prohibition dry chief Charles T. Blinn, and his partner, E.E. Enfield, kept busy raiding homes of alleged prohibition violators. Their high-handed tactics earned them many death threats. They were well-aware that county dry agents were dropping like flies, but it didn't seem to slow down their sometimes underhanded tactics.

In 1901, Charles Blinn had married Martha "Mattie" Yocum, daughter of Cyrus McNeely Yocum, the highly respected slate roof contractor. Known to his friends as Dixie, he worked as a city fireman from 1913 to 1920. For a short time, he was a stationary engineer at the Carnegie Steel plant in Mingo. Two years earlier, he decided to join the fight against illegal liquor. The Yocums were staunch supporters of the temperance movement and were happy with his career choice to aid in the enforcement of the liquor laws. In 1908, the year of the Rose Law enactment to shut down saloons in Ohio, the first Yocum family reunion was held. Temperance songs were a highlight of that reunion. The old temperance song "Lips That Touch Liquor Shall Never Touch Mine" was sung at every reunion for years to come by Albert "Bertie" Martin, a Yocum relative, and other family members would emphatically join in. Dixie and Mattie attended every reunion. She was so proud when he decided to become a dry agent, though fearful of the dangers he would be surrounded by on a daily basis.

It wasn't long before Dixie Blinn was made a deputy marshal and dry chief at Richmond. His efforts to bring down bootleggers were paying off but creating a ton of enemies. Organized crime had been in the Ohio Valley for some time, and he and E.E. Enfield were about to experience the mob's influence on the county.

On December 10, 1921, Dixie and E.E. raided the home of Pietro Bonitatibas at 633 South Street in Steubenville. Finding no one at home, they allegedly used a skeleton key to gain entrance into the residence. Once inside, they found a small bottle of alcohol and promptly exited the home. Returning a few hours later, they found Mrs. Bonitatibas alone and placed her under arrest on a warrant meant for her husband. She was taken to the

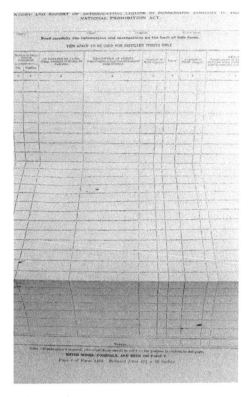

Prohibition confiscation sheet used to record all bootleg liquor confiscated during raids. *Photo by Susan Guy.*

New Alexandria Mayor's court. Unable to speak English or pay the fine, Mrs. Bonitatibas was transported to the county jail. Attorney John Nolan secured her release, and upon her return home the next day, Mrs. Bonitatibas noticed that several watches and other pieces of jewelry were missing.

Blinn and Enfield returned to the Bonitatibas residence that evening and arrested Pietro Bonitatibas for possession of alcohol. He was fined $100 or jail time in New Alexandria court. Mayor McCann of New Alexandria denied having signed the warrant, though his signature was on it. Pietro denied being given a fair hearing and was sent to jail. Attorney Nolan demanded his release, saying "I will file numerous charges against your dry agents, Blinn and Enfield, if my client is not released immediately! Furthermore," Nolan continued, "I will bring suit for false arrest and imprisonment of my clients." Bonitatibas was released, stating that he had a prescription for the alcohol for medical purposes.

Blinn and Enfield were arrested later that day. Charges of unlawful arrest and theft of jewelry were brought before the grand jury. Despite numerous citizen complaints about the high-handedness of the Prohibition officers raiding homes in the middle of the night, startling families in their sleep and battering down doors to gain entrance into residences, the grand jury did not indict Blinn and Enfield. In the face of community outrage, the pair continued to operate.

On Christmas day of 1922, Dixie Blinn was feeling good. He'd never been known to imbibe liquor before and was making quite an unforgettable spectacle of himself. Folks saw him around town early in the evening, making loud remarks and waving his gun around. He was bellowing that he was going to make several "pinches" as he wandered through the Water Street resorts. Park House's bouncer forcibly threw him out for creating a loud disturbance.

At 11:20 p.m. on Christmas night, Dixie Blinn's body was found in Marsh Alley, just two hundred feet north of Washington Street. He was lying on his back, and it looked like he'd been shot. The body had been found by a couple young boys walking through Marsh Alley. They ran screaming to a nearby resident, Raymond Clayton, who called police. The entire police department was dispatched to the murder scene, and the victim was instantly identified as Dixie Blinn. Officers weren't too surprised, because Dixie had often predicted his own murder. He knew the end was coming near. Did he choose to get drunk, at least once, before he died, or did somebody help him along?

An examination by Coroner Kirk disclosed that Blinn had been shot once in the back of the head, once in the hand and once in the back. That last shot pierced his heart and killed him instantly. With no blood found at the scene of the body dump, and nobody in the neighborhood around North Seventh and Washington Streets and Marsh Alley hearing gunfire, police knew Dixie had been shot elsewhere in the city. He may even have been murdered in an automobile.

Further investigation yielded the fact that he had been at Charles "Cocky" Walker's house on South Ninth Street between 9:00 and 9:30 p.m. The Walkers told investigators that Blinn was drunk and had some words with Mrs. Walker. He began making loud threats, according to Walker. Blinn left their residence in the company of Lulu Lyle. They ended up at Lyle's home on Webster Avenue, where Blinn remained until after 10:00 p.m. According to Miss Lyle, who was a known prostitute, Blinn waved his gun around, making loud, boisterous threats. He left her home in the company of a foreigner, whose name she conveniently couldn't remember. Police also questioned a guy named Bud Snyder, who was a resident of Lulu's house. Both Snyder and Lulu claimed that shortly after Blinn left her Webster Avenue home, they heard a gunshot and then heard an automobile speed away. The mysterious foreigner could have been Polish, Italian or Serbian. Lyle and Snyder couldn't remember. It's convenient how the mind forgets some things but is so clear on others. Where had this foreigner come from? Did he exist?

Police knew that Dixie Blinn had made himself a big Christmas night target for anyone who wanted him dead. The chief dry officer for Jefferson County had just opened up offices in the McConville Building on North Fourth Street. He headed up a large crew of dry agents who were making life miserable for bootleggers all over the county. It was anybody's bet who finally pulled the trigger on Dixie, but one thing was sure: Lulu Lyle was a central figure in the murder plot. She was arrested but released later for lack of evidence. It was surmised that Dixie was killed with his own gun after a valiant struggle. The shot heard on Webster Avenue was probably the one that went through Dixie's hand as he was being overpowered, as his gun was wrestled from him. Police theorized that he was then shoved into a waiting car, and the other shots were fired as they drove around the city looking for a dump site. Dixie's pocketbook was found next to his body, the money gone, and his pockets had been rifled. Sheriff Lucas and his men eliminated Dixie's known enemies, painstakingly checking alibis of all who had threatened the dry officer's life. They narrowed it down to the last raid he had pulled. The sheriff was confident he had his killer, but the one piece of evidence he needed didn't materialize. Without any concrete proof, the murder of Charles "Dixie" Blinn, like the murders of fellow dry agents Mike Veltry and Frank Perrin went unsolved. It was another case for the "Little Chicago" files.

Charles Thomas "Dixie" Blinn was born on July 16, 1880, in Steubenville, Ohio, to Charles M. Blinn and Laura Purviance. His widow, Martha "Mattie" Yocum, and one sister, Joyce Kettlewood, survived to grieve his death. He is buried in Union Cemetery in an unmarked grave, next to his parents. It is sad that bootleg liquor played a major part in his demise. Had he stayed a city fireman, no doubt he would have lived a much longer life than his forty-two years. Mattie went on to marry twice more and outlived those husbands as well. During those many Yocum reunions to follow, when Temperance songs were sung, I'm sure the memory of Dixie Blinn crossed the minds of all in attendance.

E.E. Enfield, the partner of fallen dry officer Dixie Blinn, had been a dry officer since the Eighteenth Amendment took effect. The forty-year-old Enfield had been Blinn's partner most of that time. Upon the death of his friend and partner, Enfield gave up that dangerous line of work and began driving a truck for contractor Harry Bates. At noon on May 23, 1923, Enfield was operating one of Bates's trucks as he drove onto the railroad crossing at Hartje's Paper Mill in the north end of Steubenville. He didn't see the seventy-two-car train that was traveling at a decent speed. It struck Enfield's vehicle and derailed the pony truck of the engine. C&P Railroad workers carried the injured man out of the truck. A doctor and ambulance were summoned. Enfield died on the way to Gill Hospital. He had suffered a fractured skull, broken ribs and a broken left leg between the hip and knee. He also had deep lacerations on his head. Just five months after his partner's murder, E.E. Enfield was dead. Was it just a coincidence, or was his death much more sinister than realized at the time? Not much was known of Enfield's background. Coroner Archie Bell located Enfield's mother in Spencer, Indiana. His family refused to claim his remains. Enfield's mother told Bell to bury her son at Union Cemetery in Steubenville. No member of his family attended the funeral. That makes the fourth unmarked grave for yet another dry officer.

CHAPTER 14

THE MURDER OF
LORENZO DiANDREA

On Saturday, December 23, 1922, Steubenville's Mayor Hawkins issued an order to the city police department to raid all known gambling establishments and destroy all gambling devices. He firmly stated that the machines were not merely to be stored in back rooms, ready to come out at a moment's notice after the threat of a raid was over. Police were to clean up all such businesses and restore order to Steubenville. This was a tall order for police officers, as citizens bent on making money from their chosen vices were coming up with new ways to outsmart law enforcement or buy them off. It was a losing battle. Good people were turning bad every day, bound and determined to enjoy the vices they were being deprived of by the Prohibition laws. Normally good family men were committing murders. The city was losing tax revenue. The Anti-saloon League and the temperance movement's hopes of good things to come with the prohibition of alcohol had the exact opposite effect. Prohibition of the vices people craved created an illegal, organized system of delivering these things. The American Mafia had been in existence for a while in this country but was now emerging in full, brazen force. Recruitment of willing persons was easy, with promises of money for doing seemingly little work. The mob knew how to lure people in, and those who got in never got out alive.

On December 25, 1922, around 6:00 p.m., Lorenzo DiAndrea was shot seven times on his front porch at 902 Main Street by his neighbor, Joe DiBacco. The shots rang out in rapid succession, drawing curious neighbors out of their houses after the shooting stopped. They found DiAndrea lying in a pool of blood, still breathing, and he was rushed to the hospital. A man named Joseph Mastro was with DiAndrea at the time of the shooting but clammed up when questioned by police. They held him in jail as a witness until they could find DiBacco.

The thirteen-year-old daughter of Joe DiBacco had been assaulted a year earlier, and he blamed DiAndrea for it. The distraught father had vowed revenge, and he chose Christmas evening to carry it out. Police put out an alert to nearby towns for DiBacco. They knew he would return eventually because he had family in the city. Meanwhile, the real molester of DiBacco's daughter had been caught and jailed.

DiAndrea remained alive through Christmas night and into the next day. Doctors were hopeful that he would recover, and he seemed to be pulling through. With seven gunshot wounds to his torso, it was a miracle that the man survived. He clung to life for over two weeks, but on January 10, 1923, he took a sudden turn for the worse and died. He was buried in Mount Calvary Cemetery on January 13. Joseph DiBacco remained at large for five months. On May 30, he turned himself in to Sheriff Lucas, claiming he had hidden out in Pennsylvania.

Meanwhile, at the Steubenville police station, desk sergeant Richard Edgerly had his own problems to deal with on Christmas night. Eight-year-old Marshall Cooper walked into the police station and told Sergeant Edgerly that he had nowhere to go. His mother had thrown him out, saying she was tired of looking after him and he was just in the way. What a jumping Christmas night it was for the Steubenville police!

Officers Hull and Conroy took the boy home, where they were met by his mother, Lucille Cooper. She refused to take the boy back in. "I just can't take care of Marshall anymore!" the mother, who worked as a local waitress, retorted. "He's in the way! Do something with him! I don't want him." Disgusted, the two officers brought the sobbing and shaking little Marshall back to the station. They were well aware of the domestic situation unfolding in the Cooper household. Lucille Cooper had had a run-in with the cops on the night of December 15, when she assaulted Lillian Lysle, aka Lulu Lyle, one of Steubenville's more infamous prostitutes. Lillian pressed assault and battery charges on the Cooper woman. No doubt, Sam Cooper, a steel worker, was spending his paychecks on Lillian or one of her girls, and his wife got a little tired of it. Lucille had a hearing before Justice Stone on December 19, when she was found guilty and paid a small fine. The situation at home, not being a pleasant one during the holidays, must have taken its toll on Lucille. Marshall was just the recipient of her mental anguish.

"I haven't got any place to go, and nobody wants me," the pitiful lad sobbed. Officer Owen Burns, known to have a soft spot for kids, having three boys of his own, was just going off duty. "That's simply just not true, lad. You're going home with me tonight, and in the morning, everything will look brighter. Your mommy is just not feeling well," Burns said. "Tomorrow, she will come looking for you with lots of hugs and kisses." With that, Patrolman Burns scooped Marshall up in his arms and took him home for the night to spend Christmas with the Burns family. He knew his wife would dote over the boy, and the boys wouldn't mind giving up one of their presents.

The next morning, both Sam and Lucille showed up at the police station, asking for their little boy. They received a blistering admonishment from Chief Blaine Carter. Afterward, he sent for Officer Burns, who brought the boy to the station. Burns shouted, "I should arrest you both for child abandonment. There is no excuse for this kind of behavior by two grown adults toward their own flesh and blood, especially on Christmas! This incident will stay with your child for the rest of his life. Mark my words!" Ending his speech by saying, "I had better not see you both here again," the chief motioned through the glass for Burns to bring Marshall in to his office. Lucille and the boy ran to each other and hugged. "Marshall, honey, I didn't mean anything that I said last night. Mommy wasn't herself when she said those hurtful things. Please forgive me?" she pleaded.

"Oh, yes, Mommy! Let's go home, please," Marshall replied, his eyes glistening. Sam Cooper shook hands with Chief Carter and Patrolman Owen Burns before he left. "I guess you know it's my fault," he said. "It won't happen again." With that, Cooper bowed his head sheepishly, and the family made their exit.

"Well, that's one case with a happy ending around here," Chief Carter sighed as he grinned at Burns. "Let's see if we can continue that streak."

CHAPTER 15

MURDER IN MINGO JUNCTION

With 1922 ending in a deluge of criminal activity and heart-wrenching stories of murder and child abandonment, residents of Steubenville were hopeful for a new year of peace. Their hope was short-lived as a fresh crop of violent murders covered the January 1923 front pages of the *Steubenville Herald-Star.*

The death of Lorenzo DiAndrea on January 11 started off the year, and it was quickly followed by the shooting of Patrolman Snider in Mingo Junction, a few miles south of Steubenville.

On January 25, 1923, after receiving a tip of a moonshine delivery, Patrolman William J. Snider and his partner, Patrolman William Hensley, arrested thirty-five-year-old Vincenzo Campano, who gave up without a fight after they caught him with the liquid goods. Campano, an alleged liquor runner, was taken into custody on Mingo's east side, known as "the Bottom." In his possession were two two-gallon jugs of moonshine and a number of bottles of wine. The officers escorted their prisoner back to the station on foot through the business district. After walking about six blocks, Campano pulled a gun from under his shirt and fired. Both officers had been carrying the liquor evidence in their gun hands and were caught totally off guard. The shot hit Patrolman Snider in the stomach, and he collapsed on the sidewalk. Campano yelled, "Don't move, or you're next!" at a stunned, wide-eyed Officer Hensley, who froze. The officers had failed to search their suspect after the arrest, which proved to be a fatal mistake. The shooter disappeared, leaving an unnerved Officer Hensley to call for assistance.

Reinforcements arrived shortly, as did the ambulance. The wounded Snider was transported to Ohio Valley Hospital in Steubenville.

Mingo Junction officers had been tipped off earlier that Campano, a known bootlegger, was en route to the Bottom with a shipment of moonshine. They had been trying to get him for some time. Snider and Hensley had been sent to accomplish this feat.

After the shooting, Hensley was ordered to the police station, where he was dismissed from his job. The chief was thoroughly disgusted by the young patrolman's job performance. "You let Campano get away!" he roared. "He just shot your partner! What the hell were you doing? You should have killed that son of a bitch!" The veins on the chief's temples were bulging, his red face burning hot. "The mayor wants your damn badge and gun now, and so do I!" Pointing toward the door, he screamed, "Now get out of here and go find another line of work!"

Ex-officer Hensley tearfully and shamefully obliged his former boss, but before he left, he stammered, "Sir, I, I'm so sorry. I, I just froze. Campano gave himself up so easily. It just didn't occur to either one of us that he would shoot. He didn't look like a killer."

"Do you know how many people in this county have been murdered since Prohibition went into effect?" the chief asked, shaking his head in disbelief. "I'll tell you—too damn many; that's how many! And most of those killers were those guys' friends! Now get out of here!" The chief bowed his head onto his clasped hands as Hensley made his final exit from the Mingo Police Department.

Meanwhile, at Ohio Valley Hospital, surgeons were operating on Snider, though they knew from experience that gunshot wounds of this type are usually fatal. The operation continued throughout the night, and doctors were amazed he had survived the procedure. He seemed to be doing just fine, and for a short time, they were hoping for a miracle. The miracle did not come to fruition, as Lieutenant William J. Snider took his last breath on the morning of January 27, 1923. He was the first full-time Mingo officer to lose his life in the line of duty.

During the manhunt for Vincenzo Campano, alerts were sent out across the river to the neighboring West Virginia counties, as well as the surrounding Ohio counties. Jefferson County sheriff Ed Lucas, upon hearing of the officer's shooting, had his entire department out hunting for Campano.

On Tuesday, January 30, funeral services were held for Lieutenant Snider. His body lay in state in the front room of the police station from 10:30 a.m. to 1:30 p.m. The citizens of Mingo and surrounding communities flooded

Grave marker of William J. Snider, Mingo Junction police lieutenant, murdered by Vincent Caparra. Located in Union Cemetery, Steubenville, Ohio. *Photo by Susan Guy.*

the station to pay their last respects to Snider and his family. The members of the Mingo Police Department arrived in full body to pay tribute to their fallen comrade, who had been greatly admired by all his fellow officers. The deceased was only twenty-seven years old. At that young age, he had already served as nightshift lieutenant and was said to be next in line for the chief's position. The funeral services took place at 2:00 p.m. at the Presbyterian church. Lieutenant Snider was buried in his final resting place at Union Cemetery in Steubenville, while the manhunt for his killer continued.

The man known as Vincenzo Campano was actually Vincenzo Caparra, a good-looking, dark-haired, thirty-two-year-old man who walked with a limp. He evaded law enforcement for a few months, until he was captured in Buffalo, New York. Authorities transported him back to the Ohio Valley, where he went to trial on March 11, 1924. On March 15, Prosecutor Enoch Stanton Pearce was making his final argument in the case, addressing the number of shots that the defendant fired. Pearce walked toward the jury and then suddenly spun on his heel, as he reached the table where Caparra was seated. "How many shots where there?" He belted out, looking directly at the defendant. "I shot him three times!" Caparra screamed, as his attorneys grabbed his shoulders and tried to shut him up. The prosecution rested their case as the entire courtroom gasped. The judge gave final instructions to the jury, and they were escorted to the jury room. After twenty minutes and two ballots, they returned with a guilty verdict and recommended the death penalty. The judge pronounced that Vincenzo Caparra would die in the electric chair.

On June 24, 1924, that sentence was carried out in Columbus, at the Ohio State Penitentiary. Vincenzo Caparra was escorted to the death chamber at 1:02 a.m., accompanied by a Roman Catholic priest. He sat down for the last time in the electric chair and said, "Goodbye, everybody." As the switch was flipped, his dry lips mumbled a prayer, "Dear God, please forgive me for…" At 1:06 a.m., Vincenzo Caparra, the rumrunning cop-killer, was pronounced dead.

CHAPTER 16

KNIGHTS OF THE
KU KLUX KLAN APPEAR

With violent crimes occurring in the streets on a daily basis and cries of political corruption ringing throughout Steubenville, citizens were at a loss about what to do about returning law and order to their city. Pleas to city hall didn't seem to have any effect because many officials were allegedly paid to look the other way. At best, small fines were levied for crimes that needed more severe punishments. The horrific rise in crime was affecting the whole Ohio Valley, with no end in sight. People were desperate for an answer to their plight.

On March 17, 1922, a chapter of the Knights of the Ku Klux Klan emerged in Wellsburg, West Virginia, just across the Ohio River and a few miles south of Steubenville. People were startled by three loud explosions, followed by three large rockets that lit up the night sky. As they looked up to find the cause of the explosion, a large fiery cross flamed up on Hubbard's Hill. White robed figures could be seen eerily moving around near the base of the cross. It was the first indication in the Ohio Valley that its first newly formed chapter of the Ku Klux Klan had been established.

On July 12, 1922, at 9:30 p.m., the residents of Weirton, West Virginia, were treated to several loud explosions and fireworks, along with the firing of a huge cross over Cove Valley. Just like the incident in Wellsburg, white robed figures could be seen moving about in the spooky firelight. People scurried to their cars and raced to the hillside, but upon arrival, they found nothing but the residue of the magnificent display. For the next few months, a few Klan members would appear out of nowhere in theaters or churches, marching through the aisles. They would leave donations with the stunned ministers of the churches, accompanied by a note, signed: "From Wellsburg Klan No. 1." They donated money to the Kiwanis for a ballpark for the kids, to area churches and to anything having to do with family values. Their sudden appearance at public events was over in the blink of an eye, and they disappeared as quickly as they had appeared. Before startled audiences could recover enough to follow, the Klan members were gone.

On March 1, 1923, a brilliant display of fireworks brought citizens living in downtown Steubenville into the streets. As they watched, three huge crosses were lit on hilltops across the river in Brooke County. They took it to mean that the Klan was now firmly established in the Ohio Valley. The crosses were a little more than a mile apart from one another, with one at the head of Washington Street, one on Fisher Hill and the third one at Archer Heights. Hooded figures were illuminated in the fiery display as the cross on Archer Heights, above the Market Street Bridge, burned.

Large crowds had gathered at various points in Steubenville. The largest crowd gathered at Fourth and Washington, where all three crosses could be seen burning at one time. Rumor had swirled that every time a single cross was burned somewhere on a hill, five hundred new members had joined the Klan.

On April 2, 1923, the funeral of a young railroad engineer named Arthur B. Remley took place at Union Cemetery. It was attended by family members, co-workers and a group of well-dressed men that the family didn't recognize. More than one hundred attendees watched as a young boy who had been standing with the unknown men disappeared over the hillside. A few moments later, eight fully robed and hooded Ku Klux Klan members appeared, carrying a cross covered with red flannel, oil-soaked rags. They silently walked through the crowd and stopped at Remley's grave, planting the cross at the head of it. It was lit on fire, as the eight robed men knelt by the coffin for a few moments before standing up. During this mysterious ritual, the crowd was hushed, as if in a trancelike state. Then, as silently as they came, the robed figures left. The stunned minister tried to compose himself to finish the service. The men were seen getting into two waiting cars bearing West Virginia license plates at the cemetery entrance. This marked the first time that the Ku Klux Klan had been seen in Steubenville proper. It was learned later that Klan members had visited Remley's residence on Dock Street the day before the funeral and placed a huge cross of red roses on Arthur Remley's casket that bore the initials KKK.

On May 23, the head of the Klan challenged Steubenville mayor Frank Hawkins to clean up the city, or, he said, the Klan members would do it themselves. On May 31, ten state Prohibition agents, under the direction of Deputy Prohibition Commissioner F.S. Evans, conducted a raid on speakeasies and blind tigers in Steubenville, assisted by the Ku Klux Klan. Twelve persons were arrested on various violations.

On July 17, 1923, the Ku Klux Klan presented petitions to remove Mayor Hawkins and police chief Blaine Carter from office due to gross negligence in the performance of their duties. The petition sited that gambling houses, speakeasies and houses of prostitution were operating throughout the city with the complete knowledge of the mayor and the chief. The petition also stated that at least eight or nine murders had been committed within the last year, and nothing appeared to have been done about them. The murder of dry officer Charles Blinn was mentioned as an example. It was also disclosed that operatives of the Klan had spotted police officers taking payoffs for turning their heads and looking the other way, thus allowing the bootleggers, gamblers and prostitutes to run their businesses in the wide-open fashion that had become the norm for Steubenville.

City officials were told that the petitions, which were signed by thousands, were going to be taken to Columbus and given to Governor Donahey. Impeachment proceedings would follow, if the Klan members had their way.

On August 16, 1923, a parade of Klansman descended on Fifth Street, and a brawl broke out with a bunch of men who were anti-Klan. Four people were shot. One of the victims was Darwin L. Gibson, a former dry officer and now a Klansman. He was shot in the back of the head, near the base of the brain. Gibson survived the shooting. His attacker, John De Santis, was shot in the left eye and was permanently blinded. Moscino Spinetti was shot through the left hand. He was charged with intent to kill. Another man had been shot, but he disappeared before police could locate him.

Between 2,500 and 3,000 people were involved in the riot, overturning cars and using bricks and clubs in the mêlée. The street was so crowded that people could barely move. The police department called for assistance from Sheriff Ed Lucas and his men. It was a losing battle to try to disperse the riotous crowd, but eventually people started breaking up and going home.

On August 30, it was announced in the *Steubenville Herald-Star* that Mayor Hawkins, after a meeting in Columbus with Governor Vic Donahey, would reorganize the entire Steubenville Police Department and form a vice squad. He had claimed that his meeting with the governor was a pleasant one, stating, "The governor is very pleased that the city is back to normal after the events of two weeks earlier. Precautions will be taken to see that a riot, such as the one we have just witnessed, will not happen in the future." Mayor

Hawkins continued his interview with the paper, saying, "A vice squad will be formed within the next few weeks. They will be depended upon to rid the city of its prostitution, gambling and speakeasy establishments." He ended the interview with another announcement that the changes would take place as soon as additional officers were hired.

On October 20, 1923, Steubenville residents were treated to a repeat performance of the three crosses burning across the river in Brooke County. From the local headquarters of the Ku Klux Klan came the announcement that this did, indeed, signify that another five hundred new members had been added to the ever-growing numbers.

CHAPTER 17

BLACK HAND MURDERS

Two prominent Italian mob families allegedly emerged in Steubenville, causing a lot of uproar throughout the Ohio Valley. From high-speed chases to gangland-style murders, it was clear that these two families controlled the majority of bootleg liquor that was being made and sold in Jefferson County. Residents feared they could be shot just stepping out their front doors, and the law seemed to be in cahoots with the criminals.

Steubenville's murder rate took a sharp rise in 1923, when eight murders were committed in the downtown area in a seven-week period. Most of these were mafia-style hits or revenge killings, and most were unsolved, even though the Jefferson County sheriff did his damnedest to bring in the perpetrators. Grand juries didn't want to indict, and prosecutors didn't want to prosecute. Allegations of intimidation and payoffs were hinted at, as criminals continued to walk out of the jail, free to commit more crimes. There was no end to the violence in sight.

On January 25, 1923, Ascenzo D. Serafini, a grocer in the southern Jefferson County town of Yorkville, received a letter ordering him to place $2,000 in an envelope in a specific location in the restroom of Louis DeRemedis's poolroom at 7:00 p.m. The letter, complete with a skull and crossbones letterhead, was believed to be from the Black Hand society. The Black Hand was extorting money from Italian business owners in Jefferson County and surrounding areas. If business owners didn't pay up, they, their families and/or their businesses were threatened. Serafini was not going to be intimidated and notified the Jefferson County sheriff's department. Lucas sent several deputies to Yorkville to lay in wait all night for someone to show up for the money. Nobody picked up the envelope, and business went on as usual that evening at the poolroom.

According to the *Steubenville Herald-Star*, Ascenzo Serafini had defied the Black Hand on several occasions when he was a resident of Steubenville. His defiance had cost him a brand on his cheek that he received when an unknown assailant accosted him and slashed his face with a knife. Since moving to Yorkville, he had continued to receive threatening letters and turned them all over to Sheriff Lucas.

On February 6, 1923, at 8:45 p.m., the Black Hand bombed Serafini's home and grocery store. The blast rocked the whole town of Yorkville, destroying two rear rooms in the home of the Serafini family. Every window in their house, as well as several neighborhood homes, was blown out. The only member of Ascenzo's family to get hurt was his eighteen-year-old son, Romeo, who had been in the rear of the house when the bomb went off. He was badly cut and bruised by flying debris. Terrified residents rushed out of their homes, thinking an earthquake had struck. For the next week, deputies followed up on tips that they had received about several strangers who had been seen hanging around Yorkville at the time of the bombing, but nothing came of the information.

Ascenzo D. Serafini died in 1943 of cirrhosis of the liver. His wife, Filomena, was hit by a train while talking to another woman in front of her Third Street home in 1947. The other woman had jumped to safety. One of their sons, Romeo, who had been injured in the 1923 blast, died three years later, in 1926, at the age of twenty-two, in a car accident.

On January 26, 1923, the same day that Patrolman William Snider was murdered in Mingo Junction, Marshal Dean Nye, a local Prohibition officer, was accused of stealing a car in Wheeling, West Virginia. Arrested and taken into custody by Steubenville police chief Blaine Carter, Nye tried to explain that he bought the car with cash from a man in Dennison. He showed the chief a receipt, but Carter held him in the city jail until Mr. Law, the owner of the car, came to town and identified it as his. Nye's receipt had a July purchase date on it, but Law's car wasn't stolen until September. Nye, who had once been the partner of Dixie Blinn and E.E. Enfield, was now a jailbird himself. After Mayor Frank Hawkins refused to fix bond for Nye, the former Prohibition officer agreed to return to West Virginia without fighting extradition.

In Wyandotte County, news of the arrest reached Sheriff Schleidlegger, who notified Jefferson County sheriff Ed Lucas to hold Nye. The Wyandotte

County sheriff had a warrant out for his arrest. Nye, alias Walter Keith, was wanted in connection with a burglary that had occurred at a large clothing store in Upper Sandusky in August 1920. He was the only one in a gang of five burglars who was still at large. The other members of the gang, including Nye's brother, Otto, were serving time at the Ohio Penitentiary. Otto Nye had once been a Jefferson County dry officer. Sheriff Schleidlegger was anxious to wrap up the old case and see Dean Nye behind bars.

On March 13, Dean Nye, the former marshal and dry officer, was found guilty of auto theft in Wheeling in record time. Five minutes after the jury members retired to the jury room, they returned with a guilty verdict. In April, Nye was sentenced to six years in the Moundsville Penitentiary.

On Thursday, October 4, 1923, Pasquale "Patsy" Barilla was hit with more than twenty slugs from a sawed-off shotgun as he tried to enter his South Sixth Street home. Police investigating the crime couldn't find anyone who heard the gunfire, leading them to believe that a silencer was used. The thirty-two-year-old Barilla lay in Ohio Valley hospital until Saturday, where he died from his wounds. Eleven shots had entered his left arm, and the others were taken from his kidneys, lungs and other internal organs. Though conscious for some time, he could not or would not reveal who shot him.

On Monday, October 29, 1923, Julius Soldini, a forty-eight-year-old Steubenville businessman, was shot and killed half a block from his South Sixth Street home, shortly after kissing his wife good-bye and leaving his residence with an unknown man. Julius had told his wife they were going to meet another man concerning some business and he would return home in a little while. After walking half a block, the two men were met by the third one. A few minutes later, witnesses claim, they had become engaged in a heated argument. The two strangers drew guns and fired at Soldini. He fell on the ground and tried to crawl back to his house. Julius Soldini received four gunshot wounds to the back and died instantly. He left a widow and three children. His death was believed to be connected to the Black Hand. Three witnesses saw the shooting but couldn't identify the shooters.

On Saturday, November 10, 1923, Ernesto Damica, a twenty-nine-year-old LaBelle millworker who resided on South Sixth Street, was gunned down in front of the Pan Handle station on North Sixth Street. He had been met there by two men who shot him four times in the back. When coroner Arch Bell examined the body, he discovered that all four bullets had passed through Damica's body. After probing the body, he couldn't find any trace of the bullets, but one had been caught in Damica's clothing. The bullet had been made of steel.

Ernesto Damica died of his wounds on Thursday, November 15, and like Soldini, left a widow and three children. Before he died, Damica gave authorities the name of one of his shooters but said he couldn't understand why he was marked for death. Subsequent reports claimed that Damica died without naming a shooter. The three murdered men had been neighbors and good friends. Each of them had been respected in the community. Authorities were unable to apprehend the shooters in any of the cases, though it was believed the assailants were hired from out of the area.

On October 10, Smithfield dry officer Charles Pearce's home was completely destroyed by a bomb, and six persons were injured from the blast. The explosion had also damaged Smithfield city hall and several other businesses and homes in town. Sheriff Lucas and his men investigated the bombing, but Pearce couldn't come up with any suspects who may have wanted him dead. "I know I've made enemies in this job," he said, "but I have no idea who would want to do this." Pearce shook his head, looking around at the debris that was once his home. "This is just too much." Lucas, with no suspects and little evidence to go on, couldn't go any further with the case. Two weeks later, at the request of Governor Donahey, the Jefferson County commissioners offered a $2,000 reward for information leading to the arrest and capture of the persons responsible for bombing the dry officer's home.

Tips started coming in as a result of the reward offer. Acting on one of the more reliable tips, Sheriff Lucas and his deputies brought in Marco Meola, alias Mauli, a man from Sebring, Ohio, as well as Phillip Bland and Gus Rambis. The latter two were wanted in connection with the bombing of a Yorkville home owned by Peter Bornes. Police were also seeking a man named Tony DiAngelo for the Bornes bombing. Mauli had been a former Piney Fork resident whose reputation was known to local law enforcement. Sheriff Lucas learned that Mauli had boarded a train at Alliance, carrying a mysterious covered basket with utmost care. The conductor's suspicions were aroused by Mauli's actions, and he kept an eye on him. After the bombing, Mauli boarded the train and returned to Alliance with the basket, but he was not carrying it with the same care as he previously had. Mauli was known to the Alliance Police Department, and they believed he was part of a gang responsible for a string of bombings throughout Ohio. While Sheriff Lucas believed that Mauli made the bomb that blew up Charles Pearce's home, he had no evidence that Mauli placed it there himself. He did believe, however, that Mauli delivered the bomb to someone else in the Smithfield and Piney Fork areas.

Peter Bornes had received a letter demanding $2,000 in cash, stating that if he didn't comply, his home would be blown up. Bornes decided not to give in to the demands of the letter and moved his family out of their home. On election night, while Bornes was playing cards at his neighbor's house, his home exploded. Nobody was injured, and Bornes didn't tell law enforcement officers about it for several days. The men involved in the bombing had discussed their plans in the presence of other people. Those people came forward and gave the names of the suspects to Sheriff Lucas.

On Saturday, November 24, 1923, the Jefferson County Sheriff's Department executed a search warrant on the property of Joe Rossi, a known hood alleged to be a major player in the gang responsible for bombings throughout Eastern Ohio. Rossi's property, located in Parlett, a little town on the Jefferson-Harrison county line, was a hangout for thugs. Lucas and his men went into the barn, where they found a large still and contraband liquor. Two men who were in the barn told Lucas that they owned the still and liquor. They were arrested and charged with violating the Prohibition laws. In the hayloft, Sheriff Lucas found fifty-one sticks of dynamite. "Boys, I've just found enough explosives to blow up Chicago!" he yelled down to his men. "Wait 'til you see this!" Lucas climbed down the ladder with part of his find, saying, "There's more where that came from." Deputy Campbell scrambled up the ladder to bring the rest of their evidence out of its hiding place. Rossi was not at home, but Lucas had no doubt they would get him before long. Upon returning to his home the next day, deputies found Rossi and took him into custody.

CHAPTER 18

DRY AGENT
LUTHER BROWN

Dry agents, under the command of John McCoy, raided a pool room and soft drink establishment on the corner of South Sixth and South Streets owned by Joe Crocessi and Frank Lefty on the evening of July 11, 1923. The raid caused a commotion outside the poolroom. Someone in the crowd was overheard yelling the word "snitch" over and over. The name-calling was directed at two black men sitting in a car at the curb. Steubenville police officers Ernest Underwood and William Hawkins, arrived on the scene. Patrolman Hawkins approached the two men in the car, asking them to leave the area to avoid further trouble. They obliged his request.

Luther Brown, one of McCoy's dry agents, came out of the poolroom, walking up to Hawkins. "Mind your own business. This isn't your raid. Get out of here!" Brown snapped. "Your fancy uniform don't mean anything here." He seemed to be goading the officer, but Hawkins didn't bite. Instead, he calmly replied, "This is my beat, and I'm here to keep law and order. You should go back inside the poolroom." Hawkins continued, "You have no authority here on the street." Enraged, Brown shouted a torrent of obscenities at the officer. Patrolman Hawkins repeated himself, "You need to go back into the poolroom."

As a growing crowd watched, it appeared that Brown was going to heed the officer as he turned around, heading for the poolroom. As he reached the steps, however, he wheeled around, brandishing his revolver. Reacting with lightning speed, Hawkins drew and returned fire, unloading four rounds into Brown's body. The dry agent dropped in his tracks.

The shooting set off a frenzy of excitement inside the poolroom, as the dry agents thought they were under attack. Most of the agents dived for cover, but one began firing wildly, breaking windows. Luckily, nobody else was injured, though one round narrowly missed Patrolman Underwood.

Luther Brown had been fired from the Mingo Junction Police Department just two weeks earlier for approaching a young girl and threatening to whip her. After the mayor ordered Brown to turn in his gun and badge, Brown joined up with the band of dry officers out of the Bloomfield court. His bitterness toward officers in uniform cost him his life. Upon further investigation, it was discovered that Brown had never applied for his bond to carry a firearm, as is required by all dry officers. Furthermore, the badge found on his body was from the state of Pennsylvania.

Coroner Arch Bell told investigators that if Patrolman Hawkins hadn't returned fire, he would be the one lying on the sidewalk, instead of Luther Brown. Bell ruled in favor of Patrolman Hawkins, citing a self-defense shooting.

Twenty-nine-year-old dry agent Luther Brown was taken back to his birthplace of Charlotte, North Carolina, by his wife for burial.

CHAPTER 19

THE PHARES MARTIN MURDER

Thirty-year-old Phares Martin came to Steubenville from Washington County, Pennsylvania, to work at the La Belle Iron Works. After a year and a half of the tiresome labor involved in being an ironworker, he decided to try his hand at fighting the war on bootleggers. He joined up with dry agents Harry Webster, Ferdinand Eoff and Caleb Harris, who worked out of the Smithfield court of Mayor W.G. Parks.

On the night of August 23, 1923, the dry agents combed the one hundred block of South Sixth Street, searching several establishments for liquor violators. They found two black men drinking liquor on the street and took them to the Prohibition office in the McConville Building on North Fourth. One of the violators was Governor Johnson. His partner, however, had escaped through a window. They agreed to let Johnson go if he would help them apprehend the bootleggers who sold him the liquor. Johnson readily agreed and proceeded to walk back toward the one hundred block of South Sixth Street to Steve's Place, where he had purchased the liquor. He entered the establishment and purchased another bottle. Upon returning outside, he handed it over to the agents. Before raiding Steve's Place, Johnson told them he would go down the street and buy more whiskey from another guy at the corner of South and South Sixth. Phares Martin was assigned to follow Johnson down the street. After the whiskey buy at Joe Crocessi's poolroom, Johnson walked back toward South Sixth, where Agent Martin was waiting for him in the shadows. Three shots rang out, and Johnson could see Phares Martin staggering toward one of the houses before collapsing facedown in the gutter. A large pool of blood oozed from underneath the fallen agent, whose gun was still in its holster. Mrs. Bell, mother of city patrolman Frank Bell, ran to Martin, knelt beside him and lifted his head into her lap. As she did so, his body began to violently shake as the death struggle took hold. She gently laid his head back down on the ground, and Johnson helped the shaken woman up as she started to sob. Next door, Patrolman Conroy had come home for dinner. He'd been sitting on the front porch and saw what happened. He ran inside for his weapon, as did Patrolman Hawkins from his residence down the block. Neither patrolman found any evidence of the shooter.

Dry agent Phares Martin died on his way to Ohio Valley hospital. According to the examination conducted by Coroner Archie Bell, Martin died from one gunshot to the chest. The other two rounds had missed him. Martin, a World War I veteran, had fought overseas in France, for which he received two medals of valor. His body was shipped back to Mount Joy, Pennsylvania, for burial, where he was survived by his mother and a brother. Just six weeks before Martin's murder, Luther Brown had been killed on the same corner, while raiding the same establishment. The police investigation yielded few clues and no suspects. This section of Steubenville became known as the "death district."

CHAPTER 20

DRY AGENT JOHN McCOY AND HIS MEN

John McCoy; his son, William; his son-in-law, Ferdinand "Ferd" Eoff; and Caleb S. Harris were a band of well-known dry officers who operated throughout Jefferson County. Their antics were notoriously high-handed.

On April 22, 1923, Charles Barton, a dry officer working under McCoy, was in Nick Kornish's poolroom on Wells Street, where he attempted a raid. He was surrounded by angry Serbians, who severely beat him with blackjacks and gun butts. According to Nick Kornish when questioned by Steubenville police, Barton entered his establishment without a warrant and ordered him to turn over a bottle to check its contents. The poolroom owner told him it was a bottle of ginger ale and refused to hand the bottle over without the warrant. At this point, according to Kornish, Barton became angered and drew his gun, firing it within inches of Kornish's head. Angered poolroom patrons jumped in and assaulted the dry officer in an attempt to protect their friend. According to Barton's version of the events, he entered the poolroom with a warrant to search the premises for bootleg liquor and was met by Nick Kornish, brandishing a revolver, firing a shot that narrowly missed him. When Barton attempted to draw his gun, someone smacked him in the back with a blackjack, and Nick hit him in the head with the butt of his gun.

The police investigation resulted in no arrests being made. McCoy and his men retaliated the next day at 10:00 a.m., stopping Nick and Rady Kornish at Fourth and Market, where McCoy told Nick Kornish he was under arrest. Kornish laughed, "You have no authority to arrest me." With smirk, he and his brother tried to push past the dry officers.

"I said, you're under arrest," McCoy repeated, as he attempted to slip handcuffs onto Kornish's wrists. A brief scuffle ensued, which drew a crowd of curious onlookers. Kornish lost the battle, and McCoy cuffed and then dragged him to the Union Savings Bank building that housed the offices of Attorney McKinley. In between the doors of the bank, another struggle broke out between the two men. Their fight nearly tore the doors off. McCoy managed to throw Kornish onto the elevator and get him up to McKinley's office. McCoy's efforts to avenge Charles Barton were in vain, as he was ordered to let Kornish go, due to the illegal arrest.

At three o'clock on the morning of June 30, 1923, the two-story Richmond home of John C. McCoy and his family was partially destroyed by dynamite. Nobody was hurt in the explosion that rocked the entire town. McCoy went outside to investigate and found that sixteen sticks of dynamite at the front of the house had failed to explode. The fuse had been lit in a hurry and must have gone out. He knew from the way the dynamite had been wrapped and placed that the work had been done by an amateur. No suspects were apprehended.

On Friday, August 3, 1923, John Maloni, a twenty-seven-year-old moonshine runner was delivering liquor to a Water Street business. Agent McCoy and his men shot Maloni numerous times as he was unlocking the door to the business. The agents dragged him to their car and transported him to Ohio Valley Hospital. Before passing away from his wounds, Maloni made a deathbed statement to hospital attendants.

"I was unarmed when they shot me," the wounded man gurgled. "They shot me in the back as I turned to unlock Alex's door." Upon hearing Maloni's statement, Prosecutor Pearce issued arrest warrants for John McCoy and his four agents. The grand jury refused to indict the Prohibition officers, and they were set free.

In October 1923, after failing to be indicted for the first-degree murder of John Maloni, McCoy and Ferd Eoff made the news once again. Both men were allegedly shot during an ambush near Blackburn's Mill while trailing bootleggers. McCoy had been shot through the foot; Eoff was shot through the arm. During Sheriff Lucas's investigation of the incident and after questioning the suspect who was arrested by McCoy's men, the sheriff determined that something just didn't smell right about the whole thing. The suspect told Lucas that he heard a shot coming from where the men were located. He said, "That's all I know, Sheriff. I swear I didn't even have a gun." Ed Lucas believed the young man.

McCoy was approached by Richmond's Mayor McCullough, who questioned him about the incident. McCoy broke down and admitted that he had been climbing over a fence in the field where he and his men were lying in wait for the bootleggers. "As I climbed the fence, my gun got caught on it and fired. The bullet went into Ferd's arm and then into my foot. It was an accident," he went on. "We dreamed up the story to make it sound better." During Mayor McCullough's testimony to the grand jury, he related the story. No charges were filed

On October 20, 1924, Justice William Downer issued warrants on McCoy and his men for the theft of valuables from two different homes that they had raided for Prohibition violations. John and his son, William McCoy, and dry officer Archie Hedge were arrested for the theft of two revolvers, a butcher knife and a KKK robe from the residence of William Sheets. William McCoy was arrested for stealing a revolver from the residence of Mehile Kornish. The hearing was set for October 27. After the charges were heard, the three agents were once again set free.

On Wednesday, April 28, 1926, John McCoy raided the home of Follansbee Brothers Mill foreman Frank Risler on Madison Avenue in Toronto. Risler was at work when McCoy, along with Armstrong and Thompson, showed up at his residence with a warrant. Upon reading the warrant, Mrs. Risler granted them entrance into her home. They found jugs of wine, beer and whiskey. The three men were searching the cellar when Frank Risler came home and entered the kitchen. McCoy came to the top of the cellar stairs, and Risler growled, "Who are you, and what are you doing here?"

"None of your damn business," McCoy snapped back, as he saw the two bottles of beer on the table. He placed one of them in his pocket. "What else have you got stashed around here?" he snapped. Risler walked toward the bathroom with McCoy on his heels. As he reached a cupboard, Risler opened a box, drawing a gun from it. He turned and fired, striking McCoy through the heart. McCoy staggered outside to his car and collapsed on the seat. Armstrong and Thompson raced from the cellar upon hearing the shot. They found McCoy in the automobile and raced him to the emergency room at Follansbee Brothers company hospital, but he was dead on arrival.

Risler telephoned the Toronto police and told them that he had just shot a man in his home. According to Risler's story, he had told the other two officers in the cellar that if they came up, they'd get shot too.

Frank Risler freely admitted to Jefferson County sheriff Allison that he had shot the popular Prohibition officer, though he claimed he didn't know who McCoy was at the time. He was remanded to the Jefferson County Jail without bond for first-degree murder.

John C. McCoy, one of Jefferson County's most active Prohibition officers, met his death at age fifty, after having been wounded three times and having survived the bombing of his home. His was also one of the longest-running careers in the fight against bootleggers, with most of his associates having met their deaths a lot sooner in the fight. His funeral was held in Tiltonsville, where McCoy had resided with his wife. He left behind his widow and five children. His burial took place at Toronto Union Cemetery, with Ku Klux Klan members acting as pallbearers and conducting full Klan rites.

The murder trial of Frank Risler began on July 26, 1927, with the long jury selection process. Over forty potential jurors were interviewed before a panel of twelve was completed. The trial lasted for three days, with Risler's wife as the only witness to the shooting of John McCoy. The jury was out for two days, and after three ballots had been cast, they came back with a verdict of not guilty. Frank Risler and his wife had claimed that McCoy drew first, and Risler shot in self-defense. The jury chose to believe the popular duo, though McCoy's gun had been found in its holster. Risler was arrested two weeks later by Bloomfield Prohibition officers after Prosecutor Roy Merryman had turned over evidence to them: the liquor McCoy had confiscated during the raid. Accompanied by the attorneys who defended him in the murder case, Risler arrived at Bloomfield court and paid his fine.

Caleb S. Harris, a dry officer who had worked with McCoy, was wounded on October 11, 1925, at the corner of South Sixth and South Streets. A couple men shot at Harris with automatic weapons, hitting him three times, though five bullets pierced his clothing. Lieutenant Fred Hull and Patrolman William Hawkins apprehended Battisto Pinciaro and John Santilli for the shooting, but they weren't indicted for the crime. Santilli was shot eight months later during a bootleg war in Steubenville.

Caleb Seymour Harris resigned as a federal Prohibition officer on January 1, 1929, realizing that the number of dry agents would be decreasing in the area. The federal probe under Judge Hough in Columbus was just beginning, and scores of people were resigning. Agent Harris was sworn in as a deputy marshal in Yorkville shortly after his resignation from federal service. During a dry raid in May 1930, he shot and killed grocery store owner John Terazakis. While serving two warrants at the Terazakis home, Terazakis pointed a rifle at the officers and pulled the trigger, but the gun was empty. Harris fired his weapon and struck Terazakis in the neck, killing him instantly. The coroner out of Belmont County ruled in favor of Caleb Harris, saying he shot in self-defense. Despite the self-defense ruling, Harris was charged with second-degree murder. The grand jury failed to indict him on the murder charge, but in February 1931, Judge Jay S. Paisley sentenced him to one to three years in the penitentiary for receiving money from an alleged bootlegger. Per an article in the *Steubenville Herald-Star*, Judge Paisley admonished him, "Dry agents like you are the ones who have brought ridicule to law enforcement." The bootlegger, Grover Allen, had produced a receipt signed by Harris as proof. After Harris served his sentence, he and his family moved to Texas, where he lived a long life and got into another line of work.

CHAPTER 21

THE MAY BLOSSER STORY

One of Madam Jennie Good's most popular and notorious ladies of the evening, May Blosser, was very well known to the Steubenville police. She had been arrested numerous times on Water Street at the houses of ill repute. She, along with Mary Wheeler and Foxy Fuller, was arrested on federal narcotics charges on May 6, 1924, and taken to Columbus to stand trial. May had been married ten years earlier to James Glenn Crum. She spent some time in the Canton workhouse before returning to Steubenville, where she took up residence in a Water Street house.

At noon on January 14, 1926, May, supposedly tired of living, slashed her throat with a razor, carving out a triangular shaped notch of skin and thus destroying her power of speech. She was found around 7:30 that evening by a man named Ralph Boseto, who immediately called the police.

Upon arrival at the scene, police found a suicide note beside the still-breathing woman on the bed. It was written in pencil in a child-like scrawl and read: "At twelve o'clock, I cannot talk. I was by myself. I am sick, no one to blame. I am a fisical [*sic*] wreck. May."

Boseto was taken to jail and held as a material witness until the coroner ruled May's death a suicide, and then he was released. What an odd way to commit suicide, let alone write a note about it! Sounds like somebody didn't want May to talk. Was she going to spill her guts to the feds about who was supplying narcotics in Steubenville? Chalk this one up as another unsolved Steubenville death.

NEWSFLASH: PROHIBITION ARRIVES AND CRIME RATE SOARS

The thirty-nine-year-old prostitute was finally at peace. She was buried high on a hill in an unmarked grave at Brooke Cemetery, overlooking the Ohio River. The view from her grave is beautiful, perhaps the most beautiful thing about her life.

CHAPTER 22

THE GRUESOME
HERRON MURDERS

The 101-acre Samuel Herron farm on the Steubenville Canton road was a huge and very valuable piece of real estate on State Route 43 in Wintersville. When Samuel died, the farm was left to his son Robert and Robert's sister Nettie. Their other siblings had moved away. It was not unusual for Robert to place want ads in the *Steubenville Herald-Star* looking for farmhands to assist him with the upkeep of the farm in exchange for board.

On March 3, 1926, William Waggoner, a milk driver for the Underwood Dairy Company, drove to the Herron farm on his usual rounds. The Herron farm supplied a large quantity of milk to the dairy, and Waggoner was there to pick it up. He arrived at the farm at about seven o'clock that morning, knocked on the kitchen door of the farmhouse and called, "Nettie, its Bill Waggoner." Getting no answer, he opened the door and peered inside. To his horror, he saw the body of Nettie Herron hanging from a rope in the dining room. He fled to the neighboring farmhouse and aroused the sleeping man and his wife, who returned to the farmhouse with him. After searching for Robert, they found him a short time later, in a barn stall with his head crushed in. Blood spatter covered the walls of the stall. They noticed that several of the stray cats that Robert had kept around the farm had blood smeared on their faces. Upon closer examination of Robert's head, it appeared that the cats had been feasting on it for some time.

They placed a call to the Jefferson County Sheriff and waited for his arrival. Within half an hour, Sheriff William T. Allison arrived at the

Sister and brother Nettie and Robert Herron. *Photograph courtesy of the* Steubenville Herald-Star, *March 1926. Used with permission.*

Herron home with a couple deputies. He was met by the three witnesses to the crime's aftermath, who filled him in on their gruesome find.

Allison's investigation turned up the murder weapon—a bloody mattock located in a corner of the barn. It had been used to split the sixty-three-year-old bachelor's head open. The investigators theorized that Robert had been killed first, as he went to the barn about dusk to put the animals up for the night. The murderer then went to the house, where he sexually assaulted fifty-six-year-old spinster Nettie Herron and strangled her. She was then hanged with a halter and rope and suspended from a clothes hook in the dining room to make it look like a suicide. The house had been ransacked from top to bottom by the intruder in an apparent robbery.

A Negro suspect who had previously worked on the Herron farm was arrested by deputies, hours after they received the call. Twenty-seven-year-old John Cook was apprehended at his residence on South Sixth Street. His arrest followed the finding of a bloodstained ball cap near Robert Herron's body in the barn. The cap had been identified as belonging to Cook by the Herrons' neighbors, who had often seen Cook wearing it while working on the farm. Despite being grilled throughout the night, Cook maintained his innocence. His roommate Melvin Woodward was also arrested for the crime after being located at Martins Ferry.

According to an excerpt from the *Steubenville Herald-Star,* Prosecutor Roy Merryman declared that Cook was "one of the coolest men he'd ever seen" under the intense pressure of such grilling. Sheriff Allison even produced the halter and rope used in Nettie's murder, allegedly placing it around Cook's neck and tightening it. Cook calmly replied, "I never saw no rope." All attempts to make Cook confess failed. Witnesses had identified Cook as the person they saw taking a bus at 5:00 p.m. on the night of the murder, not far from the farm. Coroner Arch Bell was on the same bus and identified Cook as the man who had boarded it. Store proprietor J.C. Maxwell identified Cook as the man who came into his store and purchased several items before boarding the bus. A pocketbook was found in Cook's room and had been identified as belonging to victim Nettie Herron. With all the damning evidence against him, Cook still declared his innocence to anyone who would listen.

With two suspects in jail, authorities were beginning to wonder if they had the right men. Plagued by doubts, authorities organized a posse to search the hills for more possible suspects. A Negro by the name of John Law was picked up and held in the jail as a suspect in the murder. He was also wanted in Youngstown on another murder charge. Youngstown authorities were en route to Steubenville with a warrant for Law.

New evidence obtained by police included fingerprints matching Cook's found on furniture in the Herron home. Cook's landlady turned a ring over to the police. She said he had given it to her on the day of the murder, claiming he found it out on Third Street. It had been positively identified as Nettie's ring by her former sweetheart, John Porter, who had given it to her some years ago. He had always seen her wearing it. Other friends of Nettie and Robert identified the ring as well. Police tried the ring on Nettie Herron's finger at her funeral, while attendees watched. It was a perfect fit.

Though many claimed that John Cook had worked on the Herron farm in 1924, Cook claimed that he had never worked there before. He said that he had only recently secured employment at the farm, answering one of Robert Herron's ads. Indicted by the grand jury on two counts of first-degree murder, Cook realized he would now be fighting for his life. Asked by Judge Jay S. Paisley if he had an attorney, Cook replied, "No, I don't. I'm waiting for my father to come from North Carolina." Judge Paisley advised the defendant to get an attorney immediately. The trial in the case of Nettie Herron was set to begin on April 27.

Mrs. Elizabeth McKee, sister of the victims, identified the ring of Nettie Herron. Mrs. Russell Herron, a sister-in-law, also identified the ring as Nettie's. Cook remained silent and unmoved as testimony and evidence mounted against him. Witness after witness was paraded by Prosecutor Roy Merryman, all with seemingly damning testimony.

Defense attorney Moreland argued that the state had no suspect other than Cook, so it had to make the evidence fit. "Where are your fingerprints?" he queried. "Where is your motive?" He bashed the highly questionable methods used by Sheriff Allison and his men to obtain a confession. He cited the fact that they had placed Cook on a slab in the morgue with the two murder victims. Hopes of getting a confession out of their suspect were dashed once again.

"This crime shows all the earmarks of being perpetrated by a deranged crazy man. This crime shows all the earmarks of being perpetrated by a man such as Wilbur Bowser, who had worked for the Herrons until a short time before the murders. He had been known to curse and damn them. He killed them for the sheer thrill of it," the defense attorney stated emphatically.

"John Cook has no black marks against him as a citizen of this county," Moreland continued. In his closing arguments, he said, "He has been a victim of prejudice and hatred down through the ages. It's time to give him a fair chance like any man deserves."

The Nettie Herron case went to the all-white jury on Thursday, May 6, at 2:00 p.m., and in an hour and a half, the jury returned with a verdict of "not guilty." A loud cheer erupted from the crowd in spite of a warning from the judge. John Cook smiled as the verdict was read. It was the first time he had shown any type of emotion since his arrest. It was surmised that his next trial in the case of Robert Herron would not take place until fall. Cook was not out of the woods yet.

In the meantime, authorities had picked up Wilbur Bowser, the alleged crazy man who had once worked for the Herrons and had cursed at them on numerous occasions. It was proven that he was in Canton on the day of the murders. Due to his solid alibi, Bowser was released.

Cook's second trial in 1927 led to another acquittal in the murder of Robert Herron. Cook then brought a lawsuit against Dr. Clyde Terwillegar and Dr. Caesar Sunseri. He claimed that on the day of his arrest, he was taken by Jefferson County authorities to Coe's Funeral Home and was tied down between the two dead bodies on a cold slab. Ether was then placed in his mouth and nose by the defendants to render him unconscious. He further explained that as the ether was being administered, he was told to make certain statements, but he fell unconscious before he could answer. As a result of this monstrous treatment, Cook alleged that he became ill. He had contracted pneumonia, thus suffering from permanent health issues. He asked the court for damages in the amount of $50,000. The court denied his claim.

The murderer of brother and sister, Robert and Nettie Herron was never found. Their farm went up for auction and was bought by six Jefferson County residents, one of them being Judge Jay S. Paisley, who presided over the murder cases. The farm sold for $34,000 and was bought at a time when the land was much sought after, due to the expansion of Wintersville and the route along the Steubenville-Canton Road.

Mystery surrounded the old Herron farm again on August 29, 1929, three years after the infamous double murder. According to information received by Jefferson County sheriff William Yost, a band of five or six armed men had taken up residence in the barn of the old Herron property, which was now owned by Paul Gauleski and his family. According to the sheriff's informant, the Gauleskis were being held at gunpoint and threatened with death if they notified the authorities. That night, ten law enforcement officers, armed with rifles and machine guns, surrounded the barn, but it was discovered that the intruders had left the premises. The next day, Sheriff Yost learned that the six armed bandits were actually three hungry, unarmed hobos, who had been seen walking toward Steubenville. Mr. Gauleski advised the sheriff that neither he nor his wife had been in any danger from the men. The case of the hungry hobos was solved—and without any bloodshed!

The present-day site of the Herron farm in Wintersville consists of a residential area known as Sunset Gardens and the Fort Steuben Burial Estates. The Herrons are buried in New Rumley.

CHAPTER 23

THE LITTLE CHICAGO OF THE NATION

Frank Carducci, an underworld figure who had been held for questioning in the Mateo "Mike" Veltry murder, was once again in the law enforcement spotlight when a gun battle erupted outside his home on the evening of Sunday, April 11, 1926. Carducci was entertaining family and friends after a christening. Edward Santilli; his brother, John; and a friend, Joe Derio, left the Carducci home around one o'clock in the morning. Once outside the home, they were ambushed by an unknown gunman. Edward was shot in the chest, and his older brother, John, was shot in the chest and left arm. Both brothers crawled back into the house. Derio was shot in the neck and left thigh and died instantly. Inside the house, Frank Carducci and the other men ran toward the bleeding brothers. Edward died once he reached the doorway, and his wife collapsed in a nearby chair. Adults gasped in horror, as screaming children clung to their mothers' skirts.

Carducci stepped out on the porch to see Joe Derio dead on the sidewalk. He heard the retreating footsteps of a man running down the sidewalk. Police showed up within a few minutes, alerted by the gunfire. They picked up a blood trail left by the shooter, which led them to Washington Street. A witness, who had been walking near Washington Street, saw a man jump into a waiting automobile. "He looked like he was wounded, Officer," the witness stated. "He was clutching his side, and blood was dripping on the sidewalk. Then he jumped in a black automobile and sped down toward Gill Hospital." Investigators thanked the witness and then drove on to Gill Hospital.

"No, officers, we haven't had any recent gunshot wounds come in," Nurse Sanders replied, when questioned. "You know we always report any gunshot wounds to you right away." Back at the Carducci home, John Santilli was picked up by an ambulance and taken to Ohio Valley Hospital. Cops had very little hope that he would survive his wounds. Underneath the body of Joe Derio, his .32-caliber revolver was found with one shell spent. He must have fired the round that hit his assassin.

The evening before the gun battle, forty-year-old George Jones, a marked black informant for Prohibition officers, was found outside a residence on South Sixth Street around nine o'clock. Albert Connor, another known snitch for Prohibition agents, was found that same evening with stab wounds to the neck and a severed windpipe, at the corner of Eighth and Washington. No arrests were made over that weekend in any of the incidents. Police figured the dead body of the wounded shooter would turn up sooner or later.

On February 11, 1926, someone sent the word out to all the gambling rooms and speakeasies around Steubenville, and all criminal activity seemed to cease overnight. The next day, not a gambling establishment, still or any other sign of vice could be found in town. City officials all pled ignorance to sending out such a warning to the criminal element.

In May, Mayor Cooper ordered that the red-light district was to be cleared out, and Chief Carter was to make it happen. A mass exodus of ladies of the evening began on May 22, and only women who owned their own property were allowed to stay. West Virginia authorities quickly sent out notice that none of the ladies were welcome across the river and would be run back over the bridge should they try to set up residence and/or business there. During the spring and summer of 1926, Chief Carter conducted numerous raids on speakeasies, making quite a few arrests. He and the mayor seemed to be making some progress, but it may have been too little too late.

On May 10, 1926, dry agents under the leadership of Oliver Dekins, who had replaced agent John McCoy after his murder, raided a poolroom owned by Nick Flore. The poolroom had long been suspected of being a huge gambling operation. When agents entered, they broke up a big dice game. Ten men were arrested, including Flore. One month later, on June 9, Nick Flore was murdered, his death attributed to the mysterious Black Hand. Flore's death was the twelfth murder in three months in Jefferson County.

The next day, Wednesday, June 10, Rabbi William F. Rosenbloom spoke to the Jefferson County Chamber of Commerce. The rabbi was leaving the area to assume duties in Washington, D.C., but before he left, he gave a scathing speech to the citizens of Steubenville. His speech, in its entirety, made the front page of the *Steubenville Herald-Star* and was blunt, to the point and should have shamed every person in Jefferson County.

> *If I were a young man or young woman in this city, I should leave here and go where the grime and the dirt is of industry and not of morals or blotches of lawlessness. Here is your community and it is described by press associations as a "Little Chicago." How do you like it? And it is hugely due to the fact that the citizens of today, many of you, sitting here, step aside from your responsibility to the community while authorities perform degrees that should not be recognized in any civilized court and which foster, rather than deter, crime.*

Rabbi Rosenbloom continued his timeless speech, saying:

> *Certain vices are permitted to flourish, crimes are committed and the citizens do nothing…One of the greatest misstatements is that you reap what you sow. Not so. You sow and the generations that follow reap your mistakes or your acts. That's the tragedy of it. And it is the generations unborn that are crying the challenge to you now. Are you building a city intelligent, a city beautiful, a city orderly, a city brotherly?*

The group of sixty businessmen listened intently, if not shamefully, to the rabbi as he continued his heartfelt speech, hoping that something in it would resonate with his listeners:

> *Blind patriotism is the highest kind of disloyalty. This city has its faults. I am surprised that this industrial community of 36,000 has no full-time professional doctor supervising its health conditions, nor has it visiting nurses. Its health supervision is inadequate. But don't forget that the children who are neglected today are the ones who will fill your asylums in the next generation and drain upon society for their support.*
>
> *We should have an orderly growth of the city and work spots and play spots should be provided. I haven't seen a single park in the city, although there is one on the hillside. But no places of beauty are generally provided for our workers.*
>
> *All the constructive things will fail, however, if we do not carry into our daily life the spirit of a city brotherly, a true community. There is room for Christian and Jew, for those native to the soil and those alien to the soil. Remember that the land is yours by right of trusteeship only and not by ownership in perpetuity. And all of God's children are entitled to their*

portion of it. Do you believe on Monday and Tuesday what you've said in church on Sunday?

You can gain immortality by building your city to satisfy the challenge of the ones yet unborn, immortality greater than fortunes. It will not be a selfish building-up, but you can gain the prize of immortality if you build for a Steubenville in which the yet unborn will be proud to live.

Rabbi Rosenbloom closed his stirring speech with a final thought:

This is not a farewell speech. I shall come back to Steubenville often, I hope. I can never forget it. Fellow students have carried to me headlines in metropolitan papers which stigmatized Steubenville as a "little Chicago" and I bowed my head in shame, feeling that perhaps I had not done my full duty in attempting to attack these conditions. Nevertheless, despite its glaring faults, Steubenville is a progressive little city.

The rabbi's speech came to an end with rousing applause and gave the businessmen in attendance something to think about.

The violence in Steubenville was upsetting to all of its law-abiding, churchgoing citizens. Ministers of the local churches decided to take matters into their own hands if the local police were going to turn a blind eye to the goings-on down on Water Street and other seedier sections of town. The Steubenville Ministerial Association retained Steubenville attorney William Ross Alban to represent them. Ministers did their own undercover investigating, and on a Sunday in August 1926, after the sermon, churchgoers were asked to sign a petition. The petition called for the removal of Steubenville police chief Blaine Carter and Steubenville mayor J.H. Cooper. Evidence had allegedly been gathered citing that the mayor and chief had been seen leaving a house of ill repute on South Water Street and that both men were intoxicated. The petition further claimed that both men turned their heads, allowing prostitution and gambling to run rampant. The petition went on to give the names and addresses of eleven persons who were manufacturing liquor and thirteen proprietors of houses of ill repute. Chief Carter and Mayor Cooper were put on suspension. The mayor was removed from office a few weeks later, having been replaced by Council President Sander. Blaine Carter had left town after his suspension and wasn't found for weeks. Upon his return, Carter was removed from office after serving eight years as chief of police. He was replaced by Acting Chief Ross Cunningham.

CHAPTER 24

DRY AGENT HARRY WEBSTER

Harry Webster came to Jefferson County, Ohio, from Columbus in 1923. He was appointed to the Mingo Junction Police Department as a night lieutenant. Due to the fact that his proof of residency in the city couldn't be properly established, he was discharged. Webster had been a police officer in Columbus from 1921 to 1922. Members of the Vigilance Committee of the Mingo Woman's Christian Temperance Union tried to keep Webster on the department but were met with resistance, even when a letter from Columbus city prosecutor Paul Herbert arrived with glowing accounts of Webster's two-year stint on the Columbus police force.

Webster settled for becoming a dry officer and started out working with the infamous John C. McCoy. After McCoy went to Richmond, Webster became dry chief out of the Adena court.

In August 1925, he was arrested in Columbus, having been listed as a former dry officer out of the Smithfield court. The charges stated that he had taken a mortgaged automobile out of the county to Columbus with intent to defraud. Meanwhile, Columbus police wanted him on a manslaughter charge there, which stemmed from an incident that happened while he was a police officer there. He had shot and killed a nineteen-year-old boy, mistaking him for a burglar, and was subsequently let go from the department.

Columbus dropped its manslaughter charge against Webster, and he was brought back to Jefferson County. While in the city jail, he and other dry agents he had been associated with were charged with malicious destruction of property concerning a place they had raided. All of them were out of jail on $500 bail within a few days.

It didn't take them long to get back to work. Just a few days after leaving the jail, the dry agents raided the home of legless bootlegger William Price on Wells Street. They confiscated three gallons of moonshine from the disabled man, which cost him a $200 fine. Raids continued through 1925 and the early part of 1926. In April 1926, Adena dry chief Webster started planning raids from his home but failed to show up for them. His excuse was that an illness kept him from leaving the house. On April 23, it was reported by the *Steubenville Herald-Star* that Webster was on the mend, and on April 26, the residents of Jefferson County were made aware that he was back on the job.

Webster and five of his men attempted to raid an alleged speakeasy owned by Frank Leo Nardi and John DeFrank. Both men had escaped through a rear door as the dry officers entered the building. Yorkville constable J.W. Coss was arrested by Webster for trying to impede the search. His men also placed James Fowler under arrest. The gentleman was caught with a pint of moonshine, which he told the officers he had bought in the speakeasy. By this time, an angry mob of over three hundred people had gathered around the outside of the building, threatening the dry officers with bodily harm. The Yorkville marshal arrived and, with some degree of difficulty, was able to disperse the menacing crowd.

On May 16, 1926, Harry; his wife, Isabelle; and another couple were out for a Sunday drive. Harry's wife had come in from Columbus, where she resided with their son, Eugene, to visit her husband. She'd been contemplating on moving to Adena for some time, as Harry had been living and working in that area for three years now. The couple had been having marital problems, due to Harry's indiscretion with a woman in Smithfield. While en route to Cadiz to get film for Isabelle's camera, she became enraged after seeing a road sign to Smithfield. "Harry, turn the car around," she insisted. "I want to meet your little girlfriend."

"Izzy, don't start," he replied, trying to ignore his wife. "We're just going for a nice ride. Let's enjoy it." The two passengers in the backseat tried to ignore the bickering pair. The other couple was Henry Hamilton and his wife. Hamilton was Harry's brother-in-law and a new addition to his band of dry officers. At 10:30 a.m., Harry stopped the car in Adena to give the ladies a chance to enjoy the beautiful scenery, but Isabelle wasn't about to let up on her tirade. Harry was sitting behind the wheel as the other passengers got out of the car to stretch their legs. That's when Isabelle spied Harry's .45 laying in the back seat. She grabbed it and aimed the weapon at the back of his head. The gun discharged, striking Webster in the back of the neck. Mrs. Hamilton screamed as her husband yelled, "Honey, get in the car. We've got to get him to the hospital." Henry Hamilton pulled Isabelle out of the front seat.

"You get in back," he ordered her sternly. The shaken woman did as she was told. Henry gently pulled his blood-soaked brother-in-law across to the passenger seat. Jumping behind the steering wheel, he sped off toward Martins Ferry, oblivious to the distraught women behind him or Harry's blood, which now covered the back of his shirt. His heroic attempt at saving the dry chief's life was in vain. Harry Webster died upon arrival at 12:46 at Martins Ferry hospital. Taken by officials to the Harrison County jail in Cadiz, Mrs. Webster cried, "I didn't mean to shoot Harry. I was only trying to bluff him."

She would be held at the jail on a manslaughter charge until the grand jury convened. Claiming that Harry got mad and threatened to kill everyone in the car, she said found the gun in the back seat. "Here, use this," she alleged that she said as she picked up the gun and started to hand it to her husband. "That's when it accidently went off," she continued, dabbing at a nonexistent tear with her handkerchief. However the scenario had gone down, the Hamiltons denied that they had witnessed the shooting. Jefferson County commissioner Florence Spaulding, a personal friend of Mrs. Webster, bailed her out of jail on a temporary bond so she could take her husband back to Columbus for burial. On May 26, Mrs. Webster was rearrested and incarcerated in the Harrison County jail by Sheriff Quigley.

On June 7, a grand jury failed to indict Isabelle Webster on the manslaughter charge. Judge John Worley was furious and severely reprimanded the jurors, saying they assumed the role of petit jurors instead of an investigative body. Mrs. Webster was again arrested on a charge of second-degree murder. The September session of the grand jury met and investigated her case. It, too, failed to indict her for the death of her husband, citing a lack of evidence. Mrs. Isabelle Webster was free to go home and raise her thirteen-year-old son, Eugene, but she would still have to live with the terrible act that she had perpetrated. She had killed her husband and the father of her son. Isabelle couldn't live with what she had done, and sometime later, in Pennsylvania, she committed suicide. Dry officer Harry Webster was murdered just three weeks after his old boss, John C. McCoy. The life expectancy of Prohibition officers of Jefferson County was at an all-time low. The only thing lower was the conviction rate of their killers.

CHAPTER 25

THE MURDER OF PATROLMAN OWEN BURNS

Steubenville police officer Owen Burns was a likable sort of guy. On summer afternoons, he and his wife, Sarah, could be found with their three boys out at their Wills Creek campground with fifty or sixty of their closest friends and family. They came from near and far to gorge themselves on Owen's famous turtle soup and chicken dinner.

His love of sports, including playing on the local baseball team, kept the thirty-nine-year-old man physically fit. He was strong as a bull, which came in handy on the police department. His fellow officers knew they could count on him in a pinch. The girls down on Water Street appreciated having the big, strong cop around when their customers got out of hand.

Sunday, November 7, 1926, was one of those rowdy nights down on Water Street. A crowd had gathered at Ohio Valley House. Owen, working plainclothes, was strolling around the premises when he was summoned by one of the girls.

"Owney, we need you in here! There's a guy breakin' up the place," Dorothy "Dottie" Keys yelled from the front door of the resort. "He tore off the screen and broke the window out of the side door." She pointed toward the side entrance. "Be careful, Owney! The guy's a big lug, and he's drunk."

The young prostitute was confident that Owen Burns could take care of himself. The plainclothes detective walked around to the side door and stepped inside. He flashed the badge on the back of his lapel at the belligerent young man.

"You need to leave now," Owen commanded, looking directly at the guy.

"Who the hell are you?" Albert Pirrung yelled. Burns flashed his badge again and said, "I told you to get out, and I'm not sayin' it again." Pirrung shoved the police officer. Burns, taken by surprise at the strength of his attacker, lost his balance. He fell, striking his head on the leg of the kitchen stove. Burns got up, only to be shoved down again by Pirrung. His gun must have fallen out of his waistband, because Pirrung had it and fired as Burns fell the second time. According to the testimony given by Dottie Keys, who, along with a number of other people, witnessed the shooting, Owen Burns cried out, "I'm shot!"

Dottie knelt down beside the wounded officer, saying, "Owney, is there anything I can do for you?"

"I'll shoot you, too, bitch!" Pirrung screamed at her. Afraid for her life, Dottie ran out of the room. As realization set in about what he had done, Pirrung tore Burns's shirt open and hollered for someone to call an ambulance and the police. Joe Shanley, an employee of the resort, ran to the business next door and called the police department. Lieutenant Hull and Patrolmen Davidson and Smith responded to the call. Arriving at the resort at 145 South Water Street, the three cops were greeted by the grisly scene, totally unaware that it was Burns who had been shot. Pirrung had dragged him out to the street, where officers immediately noticed that the officer's holster was empty. Kneeling by the fallen officer, Hull softly asked him, "Owen, can you talk?" Getting no response, he searched Burns's body. Checking the officer's coat pocket, he found what he was looking for. Burns was known to carry a second gun—a Harrington and Richardson .32-caliber revolver. It was still in his pocket, untouched. Hull put it in his belt and stood up. The ambulance had arrived by this time. A crowd of prostitutes and patrons from the Ohio Valley House watched as the beloved cop was loaded into the back. The ambulance sped off toward Ohio Valley Hospital.

Murdered Steubenville police officer E. Owen Burns. *Photograph from the* Steubenville Herald-Star. *Used with permission.*

Lieutenant Hull placed the suspect under arrest. Investigation into the shooting began with Officer Davidson finding Burns's .38-caliber Smith and Wesson. It was lying near a trash can with one shell fired. Police learned that Albert Pirrung was a twenty-one-year-old college student from Washington, Pennsylvania, who had recently been employed at the LaBelle Ironworks. He had gone down to the resort to see one of the girls there, claiming she was his girlfriend. The girl in question had been hustled out of the resort by friends after learning Pirrung was looking for her. This angered the inebriated young man, who proceeded to bust up the place. That's when Dottie Keys ran outside, yelling for Officer Burns.

Lieutenant Hull was still at the resort when notification came that Patrolman Owen Burns had died on the operating table at Ohio Valley Hospital. Asking the other officers to take over the investigation, he made the dreaded trip to the Burns home. It would become the hardest task Hull would ever have to do in his law enforcement career, but it would be nothing compared to what the widow of three small boys would have to face. How do you tell them that Daddy isn't coming home? Lieutenant Hull braced himself as he knocked on the front door.

As Lieutenant Hull was informing Mrs. Burns of her husband's death, the investigation was continuing to move along. Outraged by the murder of the city policeman, Judge Jay S. Paisley wanted justice to be served quickly. He reconvened the grand jury to probe into the murder at once. During intense grilling by investigators, Pirrung admitted to everything but the shooting. He claimed he didn't remember shooting anyone. Detective Tom Dignan learned from a couple of the witnesses that Burns had gotten up a third time. At that point, Pirrung shoved him down again, kicking him under the chin. It was then that he shot the dazed and confused officer.

A postmortem examination of Patrolman Burns's body, performed by Coroner Arch Bell, revealed that the officer was shot in the thumb, and the bullet traveled into his hand, which was up by his heart at the time. The bullet traveled to the heart, causing his death. The examination also revealed scratches and marks around his throat, which were consistent with the scuffle he had with Pirrung.

On Thursday, November 11, 1926, the funeral for Steubenville police officer Owen Burns took place at his home at 8:30 a.m. A service at St. Peter's Church was held later that day. He was buried at Mount Calvary with officers escorting the hearse to the cemetery. The police and fire departments showed up in full force to pay their final respects. Police Chief Ross Cunningham; Officers Owen Conroy, Frank Smith, Thomas

Grave of slain Steubenville police officer Owen Burns. Located in Mt. Calvary Cemetery, Steubenville, Ohio. *Photo by Susan Guy.*

Dignan and Ernest Schroeder; and former police officer Frank Bell were his pallbearers. The funeral procession was more than a mile long, as a huge crowd turned out to take the fallen officer to his final resting place. Eugene Owen Burns was the third Steubenville police officer to pay the ultimate sacrifice while in the line of duty and the third officer to be murdered by gunfire. Thankfully, the killers of all three men had been caught. Now it was up to the courts to make sure Albert Pirrung wouldn't get away with murder. With thirteen witnesses giving testimony about what they saw on the night of November 7, the grand jury didn't take long to return a true bill, indicting Albert Pirrung for the first-degree murder of Owen Burns.

Pirrung may have sobered up and admitted to everything else, but he still wasn't confessing to pulling the trigger on Burns's gun. On December 6, 1926, trial began with the impanelling of the jury. Opening arguments and testimony began the next day. The defense attorney argued, "If my client did shoot Officer Burns, it was under the influence of alcohol." His words appeared to have fallen on deaf ears, as the crowd in the courtroom and members of the jury watched the defendant sitting calmly at the table. On December 10, the case was turned over to the jury at 4:15 p.m. At 10:30

Albert Pirrung, killer of Steubenville police officer Eugene Owen Burns. *Photograph courtesy of the* Steubenville Herald-Star. *Used with permission.*

that evening, after twelve ballots, they came back with a verdict of guilty, which carried a sentence of life in the penitentiary. The crowd let out a cheer as Pirrung's attorney attempted to comfort his client with a pat on the back, but Pirrung stood up and yelled out after hearing the verdict, "Here is an innocent man who will be sentenced to life imprisonment." His words were virtually ignored as the crowd began to disperse, satisfied that justice was served. Pirrung was sent off to the Ohio Penitentiary at Columbus, Ohio.

On October 31, 1952, inmates at the penitentiary rioted and set the prison ablaze, wrecking eight buildings. The Halloween-night riot was a revolt against conditions at the prison, including bad food, slow mail and a dissatisfaction with the slow parole board. Six hundred National Guardsmen and 250 correction officers and police officers, armed with machine guns, surrounded the prison. Governor Frank Lausche and Warden Ralph Alvis put their heads together, trying to come up with a solution to end the worst prison uprising in Ohio's history thus far. After the six-hour battle, only one injury had occurred. That happened when an overzealous correction officer fired off a shot. He had mistaken a state patrolman for an escaping inmate, grazing the patrolman's head. During the riot, Pirrung was one of a very few inmates who aided Warden Alvis in regaining control of the prison. For that action, his name was given to Governor Lausche. On April 10, 1955, the governor announced the commutation of eight inmates' sentences. One of those inmates was Albert Pirrung. The prisoner had served twenty-eight and a half years for murdering Owen Burns. According to an article from the *Zanesville (Ohio) Signal*, the governor commented, "The offense was committed in a brothel, which at that time was openly operated. He has been a good prisoner and distinguished himself in the granting of aid to Warden Ralph W. Alvis at the time of the penitentiary difficulty in 1952." The governor was then overheard to say to a reporter, "And it might be added that brothels still are operating Steubenville." Pirrung was paroled on June 22, 1955. The cop killer was free at last. He got married, but somewhere along the way, he must have run afoul of the law again because he died in 1971, inside the walls of the Ohio Penitentiary. Albert Wylie Pirrung was the son of a German immigrant father, who owned a farm in Washington County, Pennsylvania. The family was well known and very well liked. Once again, death and loss to two good families resulted from the drinking of illegal alcohol.

CHAPTER 26

DEATH RAISES ITS
BLACK HAND AGAIN

James Vincent Tripodi, aka Trepod, was well known to law enforcement on both sides of the river. He lived in Steubenville but had hangouts in Follansbee and Wheeling. Though numerous crimes had been pinned on him by the cops, he managed to escape prosecution every time, in spite of the stack of evidence against him. His sidekick, Cosmo Quattrone, had an equally impressive batch of run-ins with the law and managed to skate away, thus tipping the scales of Lady Justice even further into organized crime's favor.

On September 29, 1925, in the wee hours of the morning, Quattrone was driving a new Chandler, loaded up with a batch of bootleg liquor for delivery, when he noticed he was being tailed by dry chief George Baynham and another dry officer, C.E. Sergeant. A high-speed pursuit ensued, beginning at the corner of Adams and Sixth Streets. Both vehicles careened through the streets of downtown Steubenville for a number of blocks. As Quattrone started up Market Street Hill, he threw jugs of moonshine out of his car window. Arch Kuhn, another dry officer who had joined the chase on motorcycle, fired rounds at Quattrone's automobile. Not wanting to ruin his new Chandler, the alleged whiskey runner pulled over, and the Prohibition officers took him into custody. They walked over to the ditch where the liquid evidence had been tossed and managed to scoop up a pint of the stuff from the broken jugs. While agents were busy gathering evidence, the Chandler roadster had disappeared. James Tripodi arrived on the scene about the same time as the roadster had vanished. Both he and Quattrone were arrested for carrying concealed weapons. Baynham had arrested Tripodi two weeks earlier on the same charge.

On February 5, 1926, after pleading guilty to his third offense for carrying a concealed weapon, Tripodi never did spend any time in jail. Father Idone of St. Anthony's Church, along with a group of citizens, arrived at Tripodi's hearing. They pleaded with Judge Jay S. Paisley, asking that he not put the young man in jail. They argued that he had tuberculosis and that his crimes were really not that serious. Judge Paisley reluctantly agreed to release Tripodi into the custody of Father Idone, after the priest vowed that Tripodi would exercise exemplary behavior while on his watch.

On November 18, 1926, the bullet-riddled body of Dr. Diego Delfino, a noted physician who practiced in both Follansbee, West Virginia, and Steubenville, Ohio, was found in his car on Sinclair Avenue. Authorities went to his residence, where they were met by his housekeeper, Rena Schrieber. She was very forthcoming with helpful information. She told them that the doctor had moved around quite a bit, always afraid to be in one spot for very long. He'd often talked about when he used to belong to an organization called the Black Hand. After he had left the organization, he received stacks of threatening letters from it. He had just come to the Jefferson/Brooke County area a few months earlier, and he'd previously lived in Martins Ferry.

The housekeeper proceeded to tell officials that a young Italian man had showed up at the doctor's home at seven o'clock the evening before, complaining of an injured arm. Dr. Delfino told him that they would drive to his offices in Steubenville as he had the proper equipment there to take care of it. "That's the last time I saw the doctor," she stated. Her last remark resonated with authorities. She said, "Dr. Delfino always told me that if I was ever to receive word that he had been killed, to tell his three children that the Black Handers got him." Authorities on both sides of the river knew who their culprit was. They soon rounded up James Tripodi. The alleged killer made bail and was released to await his West Virginia murder trial.

On January 8, 1927, Steubenville fruit dealer Nick Pellegrino was murdered as he ate dinner alone in his kitchen. He was killed by three shots to the back of the head at close range. Pellegrino was found lying face up on the floor by his wife, Lena, the next day. She discovered his body after returning from a trip to see family in Pennsylvania.

Upon being questioned by authorities, Lena told them she had only been married to Nick for three months. "I was widowed with three kids when Nick and I met," she explained. "I've been ill, and he wanted to help me out." It was for that reason, Lena claimed, that Nick had told her to go see her folks. "He thought maybe I'd feel better," she concluded. It was that trip that she had returned from, only to find her husband's body.

Sheriff Allison and Brooke County sheriff Lowe rounded up thirteen known Black Hand members, in hopes that someone would talk, giving them a clue to the murderer of the fruit dealer. Nick Pellegrino himself had been no stranger to the law. Six years earlier, he had been the suspected triggerman in the murder of Jefferson County Prohibition officer Mateo "Mike" Veltry. He had been questioned in the death of Dr. Delfino when a blank prescription with Pellegrino's name and address had been found in Delfino's pocket. Upon examination of Pellegrino's body, a letter from the estate of Dr. Delfino was found. It asked that Pellegrino please pay his bill for medical services rendered. The bill was in the amount of $162. Either someone went to a lot of trouble to set up Pellegrino, or he actually had a hand in the doctor's murder. It wasn't too often that a killing in Steubenville would leave that great of a clue. The Black Hand just wasn't that sloppy. Pellegrino's bride, Lena, told authorities that two strange men had visited Nick a few times after New Year's. On one visit, they followed Nick up to the bedroom where she had been laying down. Nick asked her to sign a document, which she did without hesitation. The men abruptly left. "I didn't see them anymore after that," she said. "A few days later, Nick was dead."

On February 3, 1927, less than three months after the murder of Dr. Delfino, a young man named Jimmy Fratini was shot in the back. He was killed as he stepped out of a cigar store. Nobody on the street could give a description of the assailant. An investigation by the Jefferson County authorities led to James "Jimmy" Tripodi. They managed to secure an indictment on Tripodi for the first-degree murder of Fratini. He made bail and was freed until his trial. His accomplices, Cosmo Quattrone, Frank DiButch, Pete Barilla and Joe Tegano, were picked up for the Fratini murder but were released later in February by Judge Paisley. The grand jury had decided not to indict them, due to lack of evidence.

On March 11, 1927, Dominic Spinetti, the thirty-three-year-old owner of a confectionary shop, was gunned down in his store by three masked gunmen. In a virtually unheard-of move, before Spinetti died, he gave a deathbed statement naming his killers. He made the statement on condition that his wife and four children would be protected. The promise was made, and Spinetti gasped his final declaration: "Jimmy Tripodi is the kingpin of the Black Hand organization. He is responsible for twenty-nine murders that have happened in this area in the past two years." With that shocking allegation, Dominic Spinetti closed his eyes for the final time. Authorities were speechless but quickly regained composure, as they slowly smiled at one another.

"We finally got Tripodi with a deathbed declaration! He won't get away this time," Jefferson County sheriff William Allison growled. James Tripodi and Bernard Castellucci were picked up that day. Frank DiButch, who had been in Spinetti's store at the time of the shooting, was arrested. He was a known accomplice of Tripodi.

In May 1927, the first-degree murder trial of defendant James Tripodi for the death of Dominic Spinetti got underway. The deathbed statement made by Spinetti seemed like a surefire case for the prosecution. On May 15, after an hour and forty-five minutes, and after taking four ballots, the jury of ten men and two women returned to the courtroom. Their verdict of "not guilty" stunned the packed courtroom. A loud, unified gasp filled the air. Judge Paisley's fury at the verdict was evident, as his reddened face took on an angry scowl. He'd secretly hoped for a guilty verdict that would surely end most of the violence in Jefferson County. He carefully scanned the jury box from his bench. "Well, I can already see that some of these jurors can't look me in the face right now," the judge thought to himself. His years practicing law and his time on the bench had made Jay Paisley a very shrewd judge of character. Not much slipped by him. Tripodi and Quattrone had gotten under his skin like no others had ever done before.

Just as Paisley had silently predicted, on May 17, reports of jury tampering started filtering in. Prosecutor Roy Merryman asked for a probe into the matter. One of the female jurors had been excused after she related that she had been called on the telephone and asked to vote not guilty for the defendant. Other jurors were questioned and admitted that they had received the same phone call.

On May 23, Brooke County sheriff Lowe presented a warrant to Sheriff Allison to turn Tripodi over to West Virginia authorities for the murder of Dr. Diego Delfino. Sheriff Allison wasn't happy about turning his prisoner over, but he had no choice in the matter. Tripodi's attorneys didn't fight the extradition, stating that their client would willingly face the murder charge in Brooke County. On June 29, 1927, Brooke County prosecutor James Wilkin brought the murder trial in the case of victim Dr. Delfino to an abrupt halt, citing insufficient evidence. Due to the fact that the state's witnesses refused to testify, the case was dropped. Looks like Brooke County got a taste of Jefferson County's medicine, and it didn't go down too good.

Judge Paisley was livid by this time, trying to figure out a way to get this thug off the streets of Steubenville. He had two attorneys look into the murder case of victim Jimmy Fratini. It was the only case left in which Jimmy Tripodi was indicted. Prosecutor Roy Merryman refused to try the Fratini case, stating there was just not enough evidence to bring it to trial. Paisley didn't want to accept the prosecutor's excuse. Nevertheless, the murder charge was dropped. The Common Pleas Court judge still had one trick up his sleeve to try to restore law and order on the streets of Steubenville, even if it would only be for a little while. On July 26, 1927, he sentenced James Tripodi to three years in the Ohio Penitentiary for carrying concealed weapons. Tripodi jumped bail and left the state. His attorneys were left stammering and stuttering excuses for their client's actions. Judge Jay Paisley wasn't amused.

CHAPTER 27

THE DEATH OF LIEUTENANT SCOTT ROE

Scott Wesley Roe was born and raised in Mingo Junction. He served two terms as marshal of Mingo Junction, from 1904 to 1908. During that time, he had an eventful career but chose not to run again when his term was up. In 1909, he went to work as a guard at the Aetna-Standard Plant in Bridgeport. In December of that year, he was shot by one of the striking workers. The bullet grazed his lip. Two other guards were shot in the same incident. Scott continued working at the Bridgeport plant for a number of years. Eventually, he grew bored and quit his job. He and his family left the area for a while, taking vacations out west and visiting family in Cleveland, before returning to the Jefferson County area.

On August 20, 1923, he was one of three men added to the Steubenville police force after the Ku Klux Klan riot there forced Ohio's governor to get involved. Governor Donahey had demanded that Mayor Frank Hawkins get the city under control, or he would send state officials to take over. Three weeks after joining the department, Scott was shot during a domestic disturbance by a man named Willie Williams in the southern part of the city known as the "Badlands." Scott was hit in the chest but managed to fire a round into his assailant's groin. Willie's wife, Patty, participated in the fracas that resulted in Willie sentenced to jail for twenty years. Patty received a sentence of two years for her participation. Officer Roe was off work for a month, mending from his wound. He learned that Willie had died later at the penitentiary after an infection set in from his gunshot wound.

Roe often worked the Water Street district, busting prostitutes and the men who controlled them. One such prostitute was a French-Canadian woman known around town as French Annie. Annie LaFleur Buckingham was always drunk and under the influence of drugs. On the night of December 3, 1924, around eleven o'clock, Officers Ross Cunningham, Scott Roe and two other Steubenville patrolmen responded to a loud disturbance at 587 Wells Street. The cops knew Annie's address like the backs of their hands. Her loud screaming, laced with French-accented curse words filled the night air. Only three weeks earlier, Officers Dignan and Schroeder had arrested her for disorderly conduct at her home. Roe banged on the door. After a few minutes, Annie answered, wearing nothing but a bruised scowl on her face. She was followed closely by Mele Wukelic, who had a .38 sticking in his waistband. Cunningham placed him under arrest for assault and battery on Annie and confiscated his weapon. The beatings were a weekly routine for the drunk and disorderly pair.

Still screaming obscenities, Annie refused to get dressed, so Officer Roe threw her into the paddy wagon in all her glory. Once at the station, French Annie never shut up, screaming at the top of her lungs until the break of dawn. She kept the good citizens of Steubenville up all night with her howling. They, in turn, kept the police department telephone busy with complaint calls. Roe would have many dealings with French Annie and her henchman over the next few years.

Apart from tussles with French Annie, life was good for Patrolman Roe. He had the opportunity to work plainclothes on occasion, as the chief saw fit. He made dry raids with other city officers, apprehending bootleggers and raiding illicit houses. Eventually, he was promoted to lieutenant.

On the night of April 11, 1928, Lieutenant Roe and his wife attended the annual Fraternal Order of Police dance at the Capitol Ballroom. They really were looking forward to the dance. It was an evening for the cops to forget about the troubles of the city and socialize with their law enforcement brothers. Toward the end of the dance, a disturbance broke out when a bunch of drunken youths began to taunt and hassle people on the dance floor. Lieutenant Roe and other off-duty officers attempted to break up the disturbance. Roe tried to get one of the young men under control. The youth shoved Roe, causing him to fall backward down the long marble staircase. Roe came to rest at the bottom, striking his head on the marble floor, rendering him unconscious. Angelo Tamburro, the boy who knocked Roe down the stairs, ran out into the alley, where off-duty officers chased him. One officer carrying a revolver fired a shot, stopping the fleeing man in his tracks. He was taken to jail just as Roe was loaded into an ambulance and taken to the hospital.

Doctors advised Mrs. Roe that, since her husband had had an operation only a few weeks earlier, he might not pull through this time. They were right. Lieutenant Roe died the next morning without regaining consciousness. Tamburro and another youth, Frank Roman, from New Jersey, were charged with first-degree murder. Charges against Roman were eventually dropped, and he became a witness for the state. Trial for the officer's slayer was to begin on June 4, 1928, but a plea bargain was reached between the Jefferson County prosecutor and Tamburro's attorney. Tamburro pled guilty to manslaughter and received two to twenty years in the Ohio Penitentiary at Columbus. He denied that he had attacked Lieutenant Roe, telling the court that he had accidently bumped into the officer, causing the fateful fall down the marble staircase.

Steubenville and Mingo Junction Police Departments turned out in full force for the somber funeral of Lieutenant Scott Roe. He was buried in Mount Calvary Cemetery. Angelo Tamburro was just three days shy of his twenty-third birthday when he killed Lieutenant Roe. He must have been

Grave of Steubenville police lieutenant Scott Roe. Located in Mt. Calvary Cemetery, Steubenville, Ohio. *Photo by Susan Guy.*

celebrating his birthday a few days early at the policeman's ball. He spent a few more of his birthdays behind bars at the penitentiary, where he had to learn to grow up fast. He served his time and came back to Steubenville. Tamburro served his country in World War II. He died from an illness on September 21, 1957, at the age of fifty-two and is buried at Mount Calvary.

CHAPTER 28

MIKE TROMBETTI

Effie Anderson was madly in love with handsome, young Italian Michael Trombetti. She was determined to marry him, in spite of her father's outspoken disapproval of the guy. Trombetti's reputation for drunk and disorderly behavior and starting fights was not lost on William Anderson or the Steubenville Police Department. Trombetti was never one to hold a steady job. He was nothing more than a hoodlum, but Effie was captivated by the bad boy's charm. On June 11, 1928, they were married. Her family was fearful that their dear girl had just made a deal with the devil, and it didn't take long for those fears to materialize.

Just a month into their marriage, Effie endured a beating at the hands of her alcoholic husband. Her parents urged her to come home with them after seeing her bruised face. Effie refused. She couldn't leave the man she loved. She assured them that it wouldn't happen again. After all, Mike had said he was sorry. He showed her that night just how much he loved her, as he led her to their marital bed. His promise to never lay a hand on her again was all she needed to hear. One look into those devilish eyes put Effie under his spell. The touch of his strong hand on her bare thigh caused any memory of those bruises she wore on a frequent basis to fade away into the night.

In September, Trombetti and his friend Dan Tamburro robbed D'Agresta's Tailor Shop. They were arrested while running from the scene of the crime. Their trial was set for November 1. Trombetti was facing some serious jail time. Effie paid his bail and secured his release. They barely spoke for days, until one night when a quarrel was brought on by his drinking. Effie picked up an ice pick and stabbed Mike with it. Stunned by what his wife had done, Trombetti quickly left the house and went to Ohio Valley Hospital, where he was admitted for treatment. After a week's stay in the hospital, he left against the doctor's wishes. Effie took him back with open arms. For the next six months, the rocky relationship of the Trombettis continued, with frequent pleas from Will Anderson for his daughter to get a divorce. On their first wedding anniversary, the couple had another huge quarrel, and this time, Effie told Mike to leave. The star-struck bride had finally come back down to earth. The unemployed taxicab driver now had no place to call home. His father-in-law's interference began to eat at him. The more it ate at him, the more enraged he became. "Effie wouldn't leave me," he thought. "This is all Will Anderson's fault! I'll make him quit interfering with me and my wife." The notion of a divorce kept gnawing at his brain, and he just wanted it to stop.

Stop it did on July 5, 1929, at the corner of Fourth and Market Streets. Mike Trombetti watched from afar as his estranged wife and her father walked up the stairs to Attorney Gavin's office. Darting across the street, he pulled a .45-caliber army revolver from his coat and unloaded on the pair, striking Will Anderson five times. One bullet grazed Effie's arm. Four of the shots went clear through Anderson's body, one of them lodging in the concrete steps. Several hundred shoppers and businessmen were within earshot of the shooting and gathered around. Nine law enforcement officers, including five Steubenville policemen and four Jefferson County deputies, responded to the scene as Anderson died. Chief Ross Cunningham and Patrolman Raymond Castner theorized that Trombetti fully intended to kill his wife.

An investigation into the shooting determined that Trombetti had purchased eighteen shells for his gun at the Beall and Steele drugstore earlier that morning. Glen Barkhurst, the clerk, had run out into the street and witnessed the aftermath of the shooting. He walked over to the chief and told him about Trombetti's purchase.

Patrolman Castner interviewed the distraught Effie. She related to the officer that Mike had not been living at home for the past week, due to their constant fighting. Effie said, "He knocked on my door at 4:00 this morning and asked if I could call and wake him up at 8:00 so he could go to work. I told Mike that I'd call and wake him up and that was it. He left and went back to the room he was staying in," she sobbed. "When I called him, he got furious because I woke him up. He started threatening me, and that's when I told him that I'd have him arrested. That's when I told him I wanted a divorce." She shook her head and continued, "That enraged him even more, and he screamed over the telephone, 'I'll fix you both before you can get a divorce.'" Overcome with the loss of her father, Effie sobbed uncontrollably, and then she suddenly cried out, "Oh God, it's all my fault!"

On Tuesday, October 22, 1929, the murder trial of Mike Trombetti began, with a jury of six men and six women hearing the case. Prosecutor Jesse George would fight the state's case, claiming premeditated murder. Defense attorney C.L. Williams was going for a case of insanity and self-defense. Mike Trombetti claimed that his deceased father-in-law had come at him with a meat cleaver that fateful morning in their home. Leaving no stone unturned, Attorney Williams further enlightened the jury when he said, "My client suffers from a sexually transmitted disease that has affected his mental capacity." Going one step further, Mr. Williams stated, "Mr. Trombetti only whipped out his revolver when he saw Mr. Anderson's hand reach into his hip pocket. Thinking that Anderson was going for a gun, my client had no choice but to defend himself."

Disgruntled sounds could be heard throughout the courtroom, and the judge banged his gavel. As quiet prevailed once again, the crowd waited in anticipation of Effie Trombetti's testimony. Gasps of astonishment permeated throughout the courtroom as the meek woman stepped up to the railing to be sworn in. She calmly told the court that she would not testify. The prosecutor stared at her in disbelief.

"Mrs. Trombetti, your father was killed. Don't you want put his murderer away?" he asked.

"Mr. George, as I have already stated, I will not be testifying," Effie replied coldly. The judge excused her from the witness stand, and Effie hurriedly returned to her seat. Mike Trombetti smiled wryly at his estranged wife. She avoided his

Mike Trombetti, who killed his father-in-law, burned to death in the Ohio Penitentiary. *Photograph courtesy of the* Steubenville Herald-Star. *Used with permission.*

gaze as she timidly sat down. The fleeting moment was not lost on the jury or anyone else in the courtroom.

At the conclusion of the trial, the case was handed over to the jury. It took only a couple hours for them to return. The foreman announced their unanimous decision: "We find the defendant, Michael Trombetti, guilty as charged." The courtroom erupted in applause as the smug killer was led away.

Trombetti was sentenced to life without parole at the Ohio Penitentiary and sent off to live out his days in his new home. Six months into his sentence, the devil got his due. On April 21, 1930, the Ohio Penitentiary caught fire, burning the area where the twenty-four-year-old Mike Trombetti was housed. He was one of over three hundred inmates who perished in the fire. He is buried at Mount Calvary Cemetery in Steubenville.

CHAPTER 29

GEORGE BAYNHAM
AND JOHN COLE

Through the Prohibition years, state Prohibition officer George A. Baynham would often partner up with John O. Cole, a dry agent operating out of various Jefferson County courts. Together, they raided hundreds of speakeasies and businesses throughout Jefferson County. They brought thousands of dollars in fines to the courts they worked for. They'd sometimes bring in $10,000 in a single month. The daring duo and their band of dry agents created a lot of enemies as a result of their still busting. Baynham's favorite method of raiding bootleg fortresses was to use a battering ram, which was often a railroad tie.

On August 20, 1925, Baynham and his men, Sargent, Kuhn and Riser, were preparing to raid the "Fortress," a well-known speakeasy owned by James S. Priest, fortified with massive steel doors. As they spied the place from afar, they noticed several men exiting the establishment with Canadian ale. Upon seeing the agents, the men dropped their illegal brew and quickly disappeared. A uniformed Steubenville police officer exited the Fortress next, continuing his rounds as if nothing was amiss. Baynham shook his head in disgust.

Having tried to raid the establishment before and failed, the agents had armed themselves with crowbars, fire axes and other Prohibition tools often used by agents to gain entry into liquor fortresses. Dry Chief Baynham, armed with a sledgehammer, approached the front door as his men surrounded the place. Baynham swung his sledge repeatedly, realizing he was only denting the heavy doors and the hinges weren't budging. Never one to admit defeat, he kept swinging and was prepared to continue throughout the night if necessary. Patrons inside the speakeasy knew the dry boys weren't going away. One of them finally opened the doors and let the raiders inside. For their efforts, agents confiscated three pints of bonded whiskey and two cases of Canadian beer.

In Smithfield, on August 22, 1925, dry agents confiscated three large stills, including one that held 100 gallons. They also seized 135 gallons of moonshine and 3,700 gallons of mash and arrested four Prohibition violators in the process.

Raids continued throughout Jefferson County, resulting in both George Baynham and John Cole being promoted to state Prohibition inspectors. In Steubenville, citizens were complaining about the raids on gambling establishments and alleged speakeasies. They demanded a grand jury investigation on raiders operating out of certain courts in the county, stating that raiders were "holding court" inside the establishments once the raids were completed and charging excessive fines and traveling expenses. Another allegation was that the raids were being sensationalized in order to obtain more funds. To avoid the notoriety and inconvenience of traveling to a court as far away as Smithfield or Adena, for example, proprietors of the speakeasies alleged that they would pay exorbitant fines to the raiders. Prohibition violators were willing to accept their punishments in order to take down the crooked dry agents. The grand jury agreed to look into the matter come September.

On May 22, 1926, dry agents led by George Baynham lined the banks of the Ohio River at Costonia, hiding in bushes as a skiff loaded with illegal intoxicants floated ashore. Agents waded through the water, swarming the boat. It was still fifteen feet from the shoreline when Holmes Green tried to steer away. Doc Ridgley started tossing the bottles of evidence into the murky water. Agents fired into the skiff, loading it with holes, but Green made one last good attempt to steer toward West Virginia's shore. Agent Richard Riser plunged into the water and grabbed the boat, tugging it to the Ohio riverbank. Green and Ridgley were taken into custody and a cache of whiskey was confiscated.

In December 1928, Baynham and Cole continued their Prohibition crusade, aiding Jefferson County sheriff William Yost on numerous raids. A federal probe was gearing up in Jefferson County, due to complaints about the high crime rate and alleged corruption of city officials in Steubenville.

While those raids were being conducted, Steubenville police chief Ross Cunningham, along with Captains George Smith and William McCarthy, conducted their own Prohibition raids in the city. Lieutenants Taylor and Brooks and Patrolmen Porreca, Underwood, Gilday, Doyle and Phillips were handpicked by the chief to go along on the raids. For their efforts, the officers took down two fortresses and a brewery.

On Wells Street, they searched a home, finding a hidden door. Entering into the secret room, they found a brewery, complete with thirty-four cases of beer, two hundred gallons of mash, bottles and two twenty-gallon crocks. The owner, Andy Spon, was arrested on a possession charge.

A fortress on South Sixth Street was busted the same night, and officers confiscated beer and liquor, arresting two men inside the building. At 133 South Water Street, police arrested Marie Hunter, charging her with maintaining a disorderly house. Another woman and two men inside the establishment were also arrested on loitering charges. Chief Cunningham and his men had arrested nine violators during the two-day raid.

On December 22, 1928, fourteen people were indicted by a federal grand jury as a result of the promised probe into recent alleged illegal activities in the county. The citizens of Steubenville noticed that a few big names were missing from the list. With the promise of more secret indictments to come, they waited in anticipation to see who else would be indicted. Among the fourteen indicted for federal Prohibition violations were Dominic "James" Epifano and Tony Solda, alias Soldina, for conspiracy. Still more indictments were expected to materialize.

On Christmas Day in 1928, a distillery was raided in Buena Vista by state dry inspector John Cole and his men. They gained entrance to it through the basement of a luxurious residence.

The owner wasn't home at the time of the raid, but a search warrant listed an H. Martin as the owner. Cole knew this must be the plant where most of the bonded whiskey sold in Steubenville was manufactured. Martin was probably out making holiday deliveries at that moment.

Agents seized bottling equipment, which they turned over to U.S. marshals. They also seized three fifty-two-gallon barrels of whiskey chips and three gallons of whiskey. The chips are said to give red whiskey its color and taste, after soaking in the barrels for a considerable length of time. Also turned over to U.S. marshals were fictitious labels and government stamps, an eight-foot-high electrical filtering plant and a capping machine. The plant and stamps were the first ever to be seized in Jefferson County. Squire Rutledge told the *Steubenville Herald-Star* newspaper that if the owner pleads guilty, once he is caught, "he will pay a heavy fine, but if he doesn't plead guilty, the case will be turned over to federal authorities."

On New Year's Eve, 1928, Baynham and Cole and their squad raided a houseboat on the Ohio River, anchored at the foot of Washington Street. Tipped off by informants that the boat housed a still and the owners were selling moonshine, the agents boarded the floating distillery. They arrested Mrs. Charles Loy for possession of the still. Her husband was nowhere to be found. Agents confiscated the still, seven gallons of whiskey and fourteen kegs of mash.

That same day, fifty-five Steubenville men were indicted, including alleged leaders and members of a large crime ring. Simultaneously, in Columbus, Ohio, State Treasurer Bert B. Buckley was indicted for violation of federal Prohibition laws, as was a Cincinnati attorney and Joseph Sperber, the brew master of the Jackson Brewing Company of Cincinnati.

In Steubenville, prominent businessmen were indicted, including Joe Guido and George Yurjevic. Joe Guido's liquor fortress on South Fourth Street was located in a building owned by Yurjevic. Eugene Fellows, a former constable responsible for turning in liquor violators, now found himself on the other side of the law, having joined the ranks of the underworld. Hiram Bishop, a former Steubenville police officer, was also looking out from the other side of the bars.

On January 1, 1929, U.S. district attorney W.B. Bartels told newspapers across the state of Ohio, "Indictments against two Steubenville persons returned yesterday by the federal grand jury here, were but a good start toward cleaning up liquor and crime there." He continued, "Liquor and crime conditions in Steubenville are the worst in the southern federal court district of Ohio. Indictments naming sixty persons from Jefferson County were reported by the jury in three sessions of this term, cleaning up the largest resorts in Steubenville." Bartels went on to say, "Conditions in that district will never be cleaned up unless there is a cleanup of the police department and city officials."

The article went on to say that federal officials would continue their drive on Steubenville and Jefferson County until the cleanup was completed. Rupert Beetham, the new state Prohibition director, met with Steubenville mayor Oliver Conley at Beetham's home in Cadiz on January 1 as the indictments hit the newspapers. It was understood by the mayor that under Beetham's plan, no mayor or village squire would ever again hear cases of liquor violations or violators. All violators would be brought to city courts and tried by magistrates of that city. It was reported that during the administration of Mayor Sander, state Prohibition inspector George Baynham would bring violators to court only to have Mayor Sander turn them loose. Few cases ever made it to police court, and Baynham reported his findings to the old state Prohibition director. Most of the indictments in the federal probe were a result of Baynham and Cole's hard work at trying to curb illegal activities in Steubenville. Each time, they would hit a brick wall when it came to getting justice.

On January 3, newspapers reported that Inspector George Baynham was confident that he would keep his job after the new regime took over on January 14. Beetham was promising the citizens of Ohio that he'd clean out the state Prohibition office and get rid of agents who weren't doing their jobs. Baynham bragged about the hundreds of gallons of moonshine liquor that his men confiscated over the years and the fortresses and distilleries they closed down. "Yeah, we've done our job," Baynham told reporters, "and we've taken cases to the county grand jury, but they get ignored." John Cole wasn't sure what he'd do if Beetham chose to let him go, saying, "I'd like to stay in law enforcement. If not this, then I'd like to work as a marshal or constable." He added, "I like the job I have now, and I'm hoping to stay at it."

On January 5, John Cole and the dry squad raided a huge distillery in a cave located between Smithfield and Bloomfield. They arrested three men inside and confiscated 1,100 gallons of mash, 75 gallons of whiskey and two stills. Running water from a spring was piped into the cave, two gasoline burners were used for heat and lanterns provided light. After Cole and his men exited the cave with all the evidence and the three violators, he blew it up with three sticks of dynamite. The men were arraigned before U.S. commissioner C.J. Borkowsi and released on bond.

On January 14, Ohio's new administration under Governor Cooper went into effect. Under state Prohibition director Rupert Beetham's plan, city and county police officers would enforce the dry laws in their own jurisdictions. If they failed, the state Prohibition department would find replacements for officers who were insufficient in their job duties. Special Prohibition agents would be placed in areas that needed serious help in cleaning up their towns.

On January 19, in the United States court in Columbus, federal Judge Benson Hough delivered sentences on the men indicted in the Steubenville federal probe. James Vincent Casali, proprietor of a North Sixth Street liquor fortress, was fined $1,000 and costs and sentenced to twenty-four months in the federal prison in Atlanta, Georgia. Ten others connected with Casali were sentenced to the Ohio Penitentiary. Casali's right-hand man, Frankie Stein, was sentenced to two years at the federal prison and fined $500. Similar penitentiary sentences were handed down to the others named in the probe. Some were sentenced to the Atlanta federal prison for sale of narcotics. James Epifano got off with a few months in the county jail. The liquor charges against Steubenville police officer Hiram Bishop were dropped, but another officer, longtime patrolman William Hawkins, was held for conspiracy to violate dry laws.

Judge Hough's actions were praised by the Steubenville Ministerial Association. It sent the judge a letter advising him that the majority of Steubenville citizens endorsed his actions. The Anti-Saloon League and WCTU were overjoyed at the huge victory.

On February 4, 1929, newly elected Jefferson County sheriff William Yost, assisted by state Prohibition inspector John Cole, conducted a number of raids in an effort to have a dry county. In Yorkville, they raided a number of establishments, making four arrests and confiscating twenty quarts of beer, forty gallons of wine and a large quantity of mash and moonshine. In Ramsey and Mt. Pleasant, two more raids ended in two arrests and two quarts of whiskey and fifteen gallons of mash confiscated.

That same night, Inspector George Baynham aided Steubenville police with raids in the city, confiscating fifty cases of moonshine and a quantity of whiskey. After the first raid, news spread around town and other speakeasies got rid of their illegal stashes.

On February 6, Sheriff Yost and Inspectors Baynham and Cole raided a series of speakeasies on Pleasant Heights, confiscating one hundred gallons of moonshine and arresting three people. At the same time, Steubenville police officers Harry Brooks, Ira Smith and Raymond Castner conducted a raid on Sycamore Street and confiscated four five-gallon containers of moonshine.

The plan to clean up Steubenville and Jefferson County seemed to be working beautifully. Law enforcement officials across the state of Ohio were experiencing the same results, due to the federal crackdown on crime.

In 1930, Baynham was reassigned to the Sandusky area, where his methods for going after bootleggers resulted in many complaints. His unorthodox method of using a wrecking iron to gain entry into residences and speakeasies resulted in expensive damages. He was reassigned, once again, to the Lorain area, where his reputation for wrecking places followed him. With the state Prohibition office undergoing reorganization, Baynham was assigned to the Columbus area.

On September 19, 1931, George Baynham was served with a $5,000 lawsuit by Edward N. Davis. Davis alleged that Baynham attacked him during a raid at his home on September 4, stating that he was shoved six feet across the living room. Davis had been arrested and fined $200 after pleading guilty to possession of liquor. Confiscated in the raid were 240 bottles of beer, eight gallons of wine and twelve pints of moonshine.

On October 3, 1931, a few weeks after the lawsuit was filed, new state Prohibition director Clarence Sears issued a statement to the newspapers. The statement alleged that state Prohibition inspector Baynham had resigned and denied participation in any conspiracy. Infuriated by the blatant attempt to smear his good name, Baynham gave his own interview to reporters, saying, "I did not resign, although Sears had asked me to." Baynham continued, "I would like to know what 'conspiracy' he is talking about and what evidence he has of such a conspiracy." Baynham went on to say that there may be people in the department against Prohibition enforcement, but he wasn't one of them: "I will insist on knowing just what Mr. Sears means by that statement."

A week later, Columbus attorney Charles Earhart, former counsel for the Ohio Anti-Saloon League, accused Prohibition Director Sears of favoritism of elite social clubs and organizations. He cited the rarity with which raids were pulled on such clubs. "Since the firing of certain dry officers, the raids have decreased," Earhart asserted. Across the state, people began a letter-writing campaign, complaining about the firing of George Baynham. Despite the valiant effort, the dry officer was on the unemployment line. He joined the Columbus Police Department, remaining there for less than a year. Tired of the corruption and political games, he switched gears altogether, becoming a successful real estate agent. The Prohibition career of Ohio's own version of Eliot Ness had come to an abrupt end. Organized crime had won out again.

John Cole had left his job as a dry inspector around the same time as Baynham. He served as a deputy under Sheriff William Yost, working the coal mine strikes. He and another deputy named Griffin were assigned to the Wolf Run mine, where their duty consisted of escorting the miners home from work. Ernest Gordon, a used car dealer from Bergholz, was parked along the roadside near the mine, yelling obscenities at the miners. Deputy Griffin walked toward the Gordon auto, motioning for him to leave the area. Gordon jumped in his car, slamming it in reverse and nearly hitting Griffin. Upon witnessing the incident, Cole ran toward Gordon's automobile, yelling, "Stop right there!" Gordon tried to speed off, but Cole jumped on the running board and drew his gun. The irate man grabbed Cole's wrist, twisting it. The gun went off, wounding Gordon. He slumped over the wheel as the car rolled to a stop. Cole and Griffin pulled the unconscious man out of his car.

"Let's get him to a doctor," Cole advised. They placed Gordon in their car and sped off toward East Springfield. Cole knew a doctor there, but their efforts to save the rabble-rouser were in vain. Gordon died en route to East Springfield.

John Cole was brought up on murder charges and subsequently indicted. He had a huge legal battle ahead of him. His jury trial resulted in a guilty verdict. After winning a new retrial, he eventually got his freedom, but it took a toll on his marriage and his life. Sallie Cole divorced her husband, citing extreme cruelty. She remarried and remained in Steubenville. After a long struggle, John finally got his life back under control. He remarried in 1940, to divorcée Ann Hixon. John worked as an engineer for the government in Pittsburgh for a few years before moving to Youngstown, Ohio. He died of a heart attack in 1955. Prohibition dry officers' lives were not easy and certainly not appreciated. These were a couple of tough guys who gave their all and ended up getting a raw deal from the people they worked for. At least these two guys lived to tell about it—unlike most of their counterparts.

CHAPTER 30

THE MURDER OF PATROLMAN RAYMOND CASTNER

Raymond Castner and Helen Marlatt married in the summer of 1926. Two years later, he joined the Steubenville Police Department. The fun-loving couple made friends with other cops and their wives very easily, throwing parties every chance they got. Prohibition, gambling and prostitution violations were rampant in the city. Helen worried about Ray's safety, but she knew he loved the job, so she kept those thoughts to herself.

Theirs was a wonderful marriage for the first three years. A few months after their third wedding anniversary, Helen noticed that Ray was acting differently toward her. His temper was short, and he appeared more distant. She wondered if he was having an affair. A wife always knows these things. She noticed the smell of women's perfume on his clothes, and it wasn't hers. After quarreling for hours about it, he finally admitted to having a girlfriend.

Helen filed for divorce, and she and Ray went their separate ways. The handsome young police officer and his mistress emerged in public as a couple. Edna James was a twenty-seven-year-old divorcée who lived in an apartment on South Lake Erie. She was known as a pretty fast woman around town, but Ray, blinded by love, was oblivious to Edna's true character.

On April 2, 1931, Edna and Ray were alone in her apartment. What had promised to be a lovers' rendezvous ended in tragedy. Edna was wounded by two gunshots to the shoulder and arm, and the young police officer lay dead on her kitchen floor, shot with his own .38 revolver.

Edna called the police department, and Officer Robert Doyle responded to the scene, along with Coroner Archie Bell. When news of Castner's death reached the chief, he and other officers responded to the murder scene. After hearing her version of the events, they concluded that Castner shot Mrs. James and then turned the gun on himself. Coroner Bell disagreed, ruling the death a homicide. He stated that the position of the fallen officer's body suggested that he couldn't have committed suicide. Though not totally convinced, Chief Cunningham agreed with Bell, and charges were brought against Edna James for murder.

Out of earshot of the suspect, Doyle whispered to Chief Cunningham, "Hey boss, when I first got here and bent down to examine Castner's wound, Mrs. James fainted."

"Yeah, so what's your point?" Cunningham replied.

"Well," the officer continued, "when I glanced over her at her, she had one eye open and shut it real quick when she saw me lookin' at her."

"Hmm," Cunningham said thoughtfully, "maybe Bell's got something there, then."

Officer Doyle took Edna to the hospital, where she was treated for her flesh wounds. She was then hauled off to jail. Her case was presented to the grand jury four times before she was finally indicted for the murder of Officer Raymond Castner.

Trial began on July 15, 1931, with a jury of ten men and two women. Edna James was the third woman in the history of Jefferson County to be tried for first-degree murder and the first one in fifteen years. She was put on the stand and questioned for over three hours. In her testimony, she told the crowded courtroom that she tried to break up with Ray that night. She claimed that they shared a joint bank account and that Ray got mad when she refused to give him any money from it. "That's when he became so angry that he shot me," she whimpered, dabbing a lace handkerchief at nonexistent tears, "I guess he thought he killed me. That's when he shot himself." The jury hung on every word, being sucked in by the sweet voice of the stylish siren. It was a Mae West performance if ever there was one. And it worked! Disregarding the damaging statements by Coroner Bell and Officer Doyle about the position of Castner's body, the jury bought Edna's every word. After a four-hour deliberation, they returned a verdict of not guilty.

True to form, Edna ran to shake each juror's hand, still clutching her lace hanky. As if on cue, she collapsed in the courtroom and was caught by her attorney, who carried his limp client outside to get some fresh air. The newly acquitted woman promptly came to, where she was approached by a gentleman who introduced himself as the owner of the local radio

Grave of murdered Steubenville police officer Raymond H. Castner. Located in Union Cemetery, Steubenville, Ohio. *Photo by Susan Guy.*

station. After conversing for a few moments, Edna James agreed to do a broadcast interview with him the following day. Strike up another win for crime in Steubenville.

Raymond Castner is buried in Union Cemetery. His death did not happen in the line of duty, but I believe he deserves to be remembered along with the other officers who have fallen. Edna may have gotten her fifteen minutes in the spotlight, but she quickly faded away into obscurity.

CHAPTER 31

MURDER IN YORKVILLE

Russian-Jewish immigrant Benjamean Oliverinski arrived in the United States in 1904, settling in Pittsburgh, Pennsylvania. In 1912, he became a United States citizen, celebrating the event by Americanizing his name to Benjamin Oliver. It was the same year that he took Minnie Lewis for his bride. The following year, they moved to Steubenville, Ohio, where Ben was the proprietor of a dry goods store. In 1913, the newlyweds celebrated the birth of their son, Aaron. After living for only a year in Steubenville, Ben moved his family to Yorkville in 1914. Yorkville is located on the Jefferson and Belmont County line. It was here that the merchant seemed to flourish. His residence on the corner of Public Road and Williams Street also housed his dry goods store.

Oliver was a politically motivated man, known for his communistic beliefs. That didn't stop him from creating a huge political following. He was elected to the board of education in 1917, at which time the Yorkville School was built. In 1921, he was elected city treasurer and, in 1923, city councilman. In 1925, he was elected for his first of three consecutive terms as Yorkville mayor, beginning his reign in 1926 and retiring in January 1932. A few months after his first mayoral term began, Oliver's six-year-old son, Leonard, was struck by an automobile driven by Joseph Jackson of Tiltonsville. The boy was taken to Martins Ferry hospital suffering from a fractured skull and two broken hips. Newspapers were calling for little hope of recovery, but Leonard pulled through.

A few weeks later, the Yorkville Union Savings and Trust went belly-up, due to "mismanagement of funds." Yorkville's share of bootlegging, gambling and murders rivaled that of Steubenville's. Mayor Oliver would have his work cut out for him through his mayoral reign. He retired from politics in January 1932, as his third term came to an end, but his voice would always be heard at town meetings.

Oliver won a lawsuit against the city of Yorkville in June 1933 allowing him to block off a section of Martha Street, making it a dead end. This angered many residents of Yorkville. A few months later, in August, he announced that he would be running for council in the upcoming election. Michael Hackett, the independent candidate for mayor, had dropped out of the race, leaving incumbent mayor W.L. McKean running unopposed. On October 24, 1933, Oliver and his lieutenants set up a meeting with Henry Coss at the Nunley Hotel. Coss, an ex-mayor and political nemesis of Oliver's, wondered what Oliver was up to.

"Henry," Oliver began, "it is my hope that you will consider running in the upcoming election. You're well-liked by the citizens of Yorkville. Your political record is spotless, and we need someone who can beat McKean."

Coss was somewhat shocked by his archrival's proposal. "Ben, you've given me something to think about," Coss replied, "I'll get back to you with my answer in a couple days." The two men concluded their meeting by shaking hand and exiting the hotel.

At 8:30 p.m. on October 25, 1933, Oliver kissed his wife, Minnie, and said, "I'll be back in about twenty minutes, dear." Putting on his coat and hat, Ben walked downstairs and stepped outside for his usual after-dinner stroll. He had walked about fifty feet down Public Road when a blast of gunfire disturbed the tranquil autumn evening. Startled, thirteen-year-old Paul Briggs wobbled on his bicycle not far from where Oliver had been walking. He had seen a small blue sedan pull up close to the curb and fire five shots from a sawed-off shotgun. All of the shots hit their intended target. The boy watched as the murder car, bearing West Virginia plates, sped away toward Martins Ferry. Oliver lay prone on the sidewalk with a palm-sized pattern of wounds in his left side, as half a dozen friends poured out of their homes, rushing to the aid of their beloved ex-mayor. Emil Pontis, who had served as street commissioner during Oliver's first mayoral term, came running from his house.

"No, no! Not Ben, not Ben!" he cried. "This can't be happening!" With a tear-stained face, Emil helped carry the limp, blood-spattered body of his friend to Dr. Lowthian's residence. He then called for an ambulance in neighboring Tiltonsville. In spite of the efforts to save Ben Oliver, he died in the ambulance, en route to Martins Ferry Hospital.

Three-term Yorkville mayor Benjamin Oliver was gunned down on Public Road in 1933. *Photograph courtesy of the* Steubenville Herald-Star. *Used with permission.*

Thanks to youngster Paul Briggs, a description of the suspected murderer's car was broadcast over the police radio. Within a half hour after the shooting, Bridgeport police in Belmont County had two men, Thomas Viola and Frank Romano, in custody. No firearms were found in their vehicle. The men claimed to be going to a picture show in Martins Ferry. Jefferson County sheriff Ray B. Long and Prosecutor Arthur L. Hooper drove to Bridgeport to question the suspects.

"This murder is exactly like the others," Sheriff Long contemplated out loud as he was driving.

Hooper ruefully replied, "I know. But getting the evidence to tie the cases together and getting a jury willing to convict is another matter."

The men were referring to a couple recent murders that remained unsolved. Three weeks earlier, Piney Fork resident Tony Ferra had been gunned down in a similar manner by two men in a small sedan bearing West Virginia plates. Sheriff Long knew the familiar pattern all too well. Oliver supporter James Magnone had been gunned down by two men in a small sedan in Yorkville on July 1, less than a block from where Oliver was shot. The weapon they used was a sawed-off shotgun. Law enforcement officers were confident that the three cases were tied together. Proving it would be next to impossible, however, and both men knew it.

Several years earlier, when Benjamin Oliver was still mayor of Yorkville, he had been implicated in the federal probe that had snared many liquor violators. In order to escape indictment, Oliver gave the names of several bootleggers in Yorkville. One of those men went to prison. This created a long list of murder suspects. Romano and Viola may very well be the shooters, but who hired them?

A few days after the Oliver murder, a couple youngsters walking along the roadway found a sawed-off shotgun just west of Martins Ferry and turned it over to authorities. Secret service agents out of Pittsburgh advised Sheriff Long that Frank Romano had a long criminal history, which included counterfeiting and gangland-style shootings. Jefferson County authorities were confident they had their killers. They hoped that the gun found near Martins Ferry would yield the proof they needed for a conviction.

Sheriff Long learned that Michael Hackett had withdrawn from the upcoming Yorkville mayor's race the previous Monday because he'd received several menacing letters. The letters contained threats of bodily harm to him and his family if he didn't withdraw from the mayoral race. Rumors of Oliver being tied to the numbers racket began to surface. Jefferson County prosecutor Arthur Hooper found that revelation hard to believe.

"I worked as Yorkville solicitor during Ben Oliver's first term as mayor," he confided to Sheriff Long. "I never heard of him being tied to anything illegal. He was an honest man." He continued, "It looks like somebody's trying to muddy his good name to throw us off track."

The sheriff agreed. "Same old tricks, different crime," he muttered.

On February 24, 1934, jury selection began in the first-degree murder trial of Frank Romano, with seventy-five prospective jurors called. Judge J.C. Oglevee, sitting in for Judge Jay Paisley, who was ill, ordered that the courtroom doors be locked. On the fourth day, February 28, one of the jurors failed to appear. Judge Oglevee ordered Sheriff Long to find the juror immediately. The sheriff and his deputies scoured the courthouse and made telephone calls, while counsel and clerks poured into the hallway to await the sheriff's return. Judge Oglevee suddenly realized that he and court stenographer Agnes Donnan were the only ones in the courtroom with the murder defendant, Frank Romano. Quickly, he told the young woman, "Miss Donnan, I am deputizing you to watch the prisoner. There are no deputies in the courtroom. Mr. Romano could walk free, if he wanted to." He ended with, "So don't take your eyes off of him, until the sheriff returns." The startled stenographer, now Jefferson County's first female deputy, diligently kept a watchful eye over her prisoner. Her law enforcement career lasted for three long minutes. She heaved a huge sigh of relief upon seeing a uniformed deputy return to the courtroom. The missing juror had been located.

On March 1, 1934, the jury and Romano, accompanied by Sheriff Long and Deputy William Westlake, traveled to Yorkville. Their first stop was the site where murder victim Benjamin Oliver was shot on Public Road. The jury was made aware of the location of Oliver's home, his store and the nearby theater. The junction of Martha Street, Public Road and Sinclair Avenue were also pointed out. They were driven down Sinclair to where it joined Route 7 at the Yorkville Airport, proceeding a half mile up Glen Run Road to the place where it crosses the creek. It was here on the banks of the creek that the sawed-off shotgun was found by the young boys. Throughout the trip, Romano laughed and joked, telling the sheriff about his family back in Pittsburgh. He maintained a nonchalant demeanor, all the while keeping an eye on the reactions of the jurors.

The caravan continued toward Bridgeport, where the two men had been taken into custody by Patrolman Delbrugge. He had stationed himself at the end of the Aetnaville Bridge after receiving the call from Yorkville about the fleeing suspects. A few minutes later, he had noticed the small blue sedan traveling down Lincoln Avenue. He pulled the men over near Bridge Street in front of the Howard Wilson furniture store. They offered no resistance as he questioned them and placed them under arrest. It was here, in front of the furniture store, that the jury ended its fact-finding tour.

The next day, March 2, Coroner Charles Wells, the state's first witness, produced the lead slug taken from Oliver's body and the bloodstained coat that he'd been wearing. He related facts pertaining to the autopsy.

Next to testify was Mrs. Florence Mackey, wife of the theater operator. Mrs. Mackey had been seated in the ticket booth, at the corner of Sinclair and Public Road, just a short distance from the murder scene. She was startled by what she thought was a car backfiring and looked out in time to see a blue sedan speeding down Sinclair Avenue. It wasn't until a few minutes later that she realized a shooting had occurred.

Thomas Clossor, an ambulance driver for Burford's Funeral Home, testified that he had driven the ambulance that night, taking Oliver to Martins Ferry Hospital. The ride to the hospital had taken about seven to eight minutes. Hospital personnel had declared the former mayor dead at 8:45 p.m.

Marshal Leo Ricker testified that he and his wife were walking along Market Street in front of the city building when the shots rang out. Due to the number of empty lots between the two streets, he clearly saw the blue sedan speed down Sinclair from his vantage point. The couple rounded the corner and noticed the gathering crowd. Ben Oliver was lying on the sidewalk. Ricker called the Bridgeport police from the home of Mrs. Novelle Kull. Upon further testimony, it was learned that Ricker had also come into possession of the murder weapon. It had been turned over to him by the youths who had found it on the creek bank.

Mrs. Oliver's testimony was heart-wrenching. She broke down into tears at the first mention of her husband's name but still managed to testify. "I never heard my husband mention the names Romano or Viola," she replied to Prosecutor Hooper. "I don't know of any enemies my husband might have had, but he always carried a gun with him." After the bereaved widow answered a few more questions, she was helped from the witness stand by her son.

As the trial continued, Romano's defense attorneys, Hugo Alexander and John Gardner, interjected at varying times. Attorney Alexander stated, "Our witnesses will testify to seeing a mysterious green sedan leaving the murder scene. It traveled up over the hill toward Dillonvale and Mount Pleasant." Their ploy was intended to create doubt in the minds of the jurors.

The trial of Frank Romano ended on March 8. After deliberating for forty-six minutes and casting two ballots, the jury came back with the unanimous vote of acquittal. The nine-day-long murder trial had ended in bitter disappointment. Romano showed no emotion after the reading of the verdict. The rising murmur among courtroom onlookers was quickly quieted by Bailiff William

Frank Romano (above) was acquitted of murdering ex-Yorkville mayor Benjamin Oliver. *Photo courtesy of the* Steubenville Herald-Star. *Used with permission.*

Thomas Viola (right), accused of murdering ex-Yorkville mayor Benjamin Oliver, was shot by his brother during a domestic dispute before he could go to trial. *Photo courtesy of the* Steubenville Herald-Star. *Used with permission.*

Fellows. Romano's wife, who had been strategically seated in the front row with their three children, gasped as the verdict was read. Her freed husband rushed to embrace his family as disgusted onlookers left the courtroom.

Following the acquittal of Romano, Viola's bond was reduced from $16,000 to $3,000. He was released from the Jefferson County jail and his trial postponed indefinitely. On May 9, 1934, Thomas Viola was shot and killed by his brother, Carmelo, during a family quarrel at their home across the river in Follansbee, West Virginia. Another unsolved murder was added to Jefferson County's ever-growing list.

CHAPTER 32

PROHIBITION IS
REPEALED

In December 1933, just a few months after Oliver's murder, the
Eighteenth Amendment to the Constitution (the "Prohibition Law")
was repealed by the ratification of the Twenty-first Amendment. The hope
that the prohibition of saloons would restore family values and keep men
from blowing their money on liquor had failed miserably. In fact, it had
the exact opposite effect. Organized crime flourished, creating monsters
out of seemingly good, churchgoing people. Thousands of underground
speakeasies had sprouted around the countryside. The repeal of Prohibition
could never bring back all of those people whose lives had been destroyed
or the men who were gunned down in the process. Millions of dollars were
made by the vices that drew people in. The criminal element wasn't about to
give up that cash flow. Prostitution, booze, gambling and drug trafficking had
been around for a long time, but Prohibition was the catalyst that brought
out the demons in people who craved those vices. The old saying "People
want what they can't have" comes to mind. The "Dirty Thirties" were just
beginning, and organized crime was here to stay.

In 1938, Cosimo "Cosmo" Quattrone's gambling room on Market Street
in the rear of his Rex Cigar store was raided, for which he paid a $300 fine.
After moving to Florida, he turned the operation over to Joe Quattrone. In
1940, the establishment was raided again. The large gambling room had a
bulletproof office, located in the rear of the room and accessible by a short
flight of stairs. Men in the office could see everything that was going on
in the room. Inside the office, raiders found sawed-off shotguns and other

weapons. Six people were arrested, including Joe Quattrone. All men pled guilty before Judge Downer. Quattrone paid a $50 fine, and the other men paid fines of $25.

Episodes of this nature would continue for years to come. Around 1938, a teenage girl, born in Kentucky and raised near Cincinnati, would come into the Ohio Valley. She would become a valuable asset to the mob and a dear friend to law enforcement. She was in training to take over for the retiring madam of Water Street. She would become known as Madam Judy Jordan.

PART III
PICTURES OF STEUBENVILLE AND NOTABLE GRAVES IN UNION CEMETERY

Opposite, top: Jefferson County Courthouse in Steubenville, Ohio, as it looks today. *Photograph courtesy of David Guy Jr. Used with permission.*

Opposite, bottom: Scales of Justice atop the Jefferson County Courthouse in Steubenville, Ohio. *Photograph courtesy of David Guy Jr. Used with permission.*

View of the Panhandle Bridge and Veterans Memorial Bridge, which connect Steubenville, Ohio, to Weirton, West Virginia. *Photo courtesy of David Guy Jr.*

Old Steubenville Police Station. *Photo by Susan Guy.*

New Steubenville Municipal Building and Jefferson County Courthouse. *Photo by Susan Guy.*

Jefferson County Justice Center. *Photo by Susan Guy.*

Jefferson County's Bicentennial Bell. *Photo courtesy of David Guy Jr.*

Union cemetery monument of Steubenville native Edwin Stanton Fickes, architect and vice-president of Alcoa Aluminum. His design of the Alcoa Edgewater Works in New Jersey was on the National Registry of Historic Places until it was demolished. *Photo by Susan Guy.*

Old Union Cemetery office. *Photo by Susan Guy.*

Resting place of Steubenville native Jimmy "the Greek" Snyder, famous Las Vegas oddsmaker, in Union Cemetery. *Photo by Susan Guy.*

Grave marker of Moses Fleetwood Walker, first black player in Major League Baseball. Located in Union Cemetery. *Photo by Susan Guy.*

BIBLIOGRAPHY

Ancestry.com

Brand, Richard. "Death Plays a Wedding March." *True Detective Magazine*, January 1936.

FamilySearch.org

NewspaperArchive.com

Steubenville City Directories

Steubenville Herald-Star editions from 1900 through 1940

Steubenville Weekly Gazette from 1875 to 1900

United States census records

INDEX

INDEX

ABOUT THE AUTHOR

Photo by Susan Guy.

S usan M. Guy was born and raised in Jefferson County, Ohio. Following in the footsteps of her father, a retired Wintersville police captain, Susan served as a police officer on the Cross Creek Township Police Department for fifteen years, achieving the rank of sergeant. Since 1994, she has been employed by the State of Ohio as a correctional officer. Her hobbies include genealogy and writing, which she often combines to tell stories of people long since passed, believing that everyone deserves to be remembered. She is a member of the Fort Steuben Chapter of the Daughters of the American Revolution and is the public relations director for the Tri State Writers Society. She credits the Tri State Writers Society and its president, author Karina Garrison, for asking her to write a short story assignment on prostitution in Steubenville. The story took on a life of its own as the urge to dig for more information took over. The result is this book.

CPSIA information can be obtained
at www.ICGtesting.com
Printed in the USA
BVHW040232230420
578217BV00007BA/59